The Ghost Hunter's Field Guide

Gettysburg
& Beyond

Haunted Sites Revealed!
Theories Explained!
Gravesites Located!
Procedures Explicated!
Warnings Issued!

by
Mark Nesbitt
Author of
The Ghosts of Gettysburg Series

Second Chance Publications
Gettysburg, PA 17325

Printed and bound in the United States of America

Published by *SECOND CHANCE PUBLICATIONS*
P.O. Box 3126
Gettysburg, PA. 17325

ISBN-10: 0-9752836-1-8
ISBN-13: 978-0-9752836-1-5

Photos by the author unless otherwise credited.

To Tim

Somewhere in the Ether

CONTENTS

ACKNOWLEDGMENTS

I would like to thank the following people for their assistance, encouragement, and expertise in developing this book: Katie Bowman, Dr. Charles Emmons, Joe Farrell, Rick Fisher, David Livingston, and Shelley Sykes. Especially, I would like to acknowledge my wife, Carol, for her tireless efforts and support in the development and production of this work.

PREFACE

It was a rare invitation we received: to do a scientific investigation in search of the remnants—electromagnetic, visual, tactile, or auditory—of someone associated with the ancient building; who lived, died, and mysteriously, may remain, in whatever form, within the structure.

In the nearly four decades of collecting tales of the lurking dead at Gettysburg, I have had occasion to actually come in contact with the physical manifestations of the creatures consigned long ago, by happenstance or human hand, to their graves. It is one thing to inhale the odor of those freshly killed, then to have it just as suddenly vanish from your olfactory system; or to feel the horrible icy chill down the nape of your neck in spite of the heat of a summer's night; or to witness the wispy forms coagulate from the dark, dreary nothingness of night along a patch of battlefield road, only to have them suddenly dematerialize before your eyes.

But it is another horrifying thing entirely—an experience that lends a more frightful aspect to "ghost hunting" because of its potential for the unsought, most intimate knowledge of the deceased—when they speak to you!

And so it was with mild anxiety that, upon a certain dark evening, I entered the birth-house of a young lady of mid-nineteenth century Gettysburg, dead for some 140 years.

The edifice was the birthplace of a girl who sadly remains more famous for her death than her life; Mary Virginia "Jennie" Wade was born in this wood-frame structure on Baltimore Street, in Gettysburg.

Jennie's life of 20 years was lived mainly within a triangle of houses not more than a few hundred yards on a side. She wandered outside the triangle to shop around the main square of Gettysburg; she may have gone to the local jail on High Street or the Alms House just north of Gettysburg to visit her hard-luck father. If she got to any of the local big cities, like Harrisburg or Baltimore, it would be a surprise. She grew up in a frame house on Breckenridge Street. She was killed by a stray Confederate bullet, while baking bread for Union soldiers, in a brick house on Baltimore Street. She was born in the small wooden house I was about to spend an eerie evening investigating.

The other investigators and I had moved through the house taking photos with infrared lights and videotaping certain rooms with historical import. I had left the video camera running in the alleged birth room. We were in one of the front rooms. It was—no pun intended—deathly quiet.

I held my Panasonic digital recorder very still. It was set on "voice activation." I turned the machine on. I addressed the name on the ownership records I had researched: "John Pfoutz, are you here?"

In complete and total silence, with the only explanation one to produce unbelief and dread, the numbers on the recorder began to move.

Something, unheard, unseen—and unreal—was responding . . .

INTRODUCTION

The mystery of war enshrouds the deeper mystery of death.
—William Manchester, *Goodbye, Darkness*

Since the publication in 1991 of *Ghosts of Gettysburg: Spirits, Apparitions and Haunted Places of the Battlefield* and the subsequent printings of numerous additional volumes, a new way of looking at Gettysburg is emerging.

Instead of a list of battle actions to be memorized (or become confused over), or names of long-deceased officers or boring dates and times, Gettysburg has become a place of mysterious, sometimes unexplainable stories of out-of-place noises and smells, of sights that are out-of-time, and of strange experiences in what should just be a jumble of rocks or a benign open field.

With the vast amounts of anecdotal proof that there *is* paranormal activity on the battlefield and in the town, Gettysburg has become a "spirit-place;" a place where the visitor may gain a different—and broader—experience other than that which is provided between the pages of a history book.

*   *   *

What happens after humans die is a question that embraces, yet goes far beyond, three momentous days in July in the middle of the 19th Century in one small American town. It relates directly to the question asked by our ancestors at least 70,000 years ago when they buried those sleepers, who would not awake, with food and weapons for the next journey upon which they were about to depart.

It is a question that today inevitably forces itself, unbidden, into our own personal lives:

What happens to *me* when I die?

The study of ghosts at Gettysburg has taken the place from a symbol of the greatest battle in the most tragic war our nation has ever been engaged in, to a symbol of a much more universal theme:

What happens after life ends?

And Gettysburg, long a place for solemn contemplation of martial deeds done by Union and Confederate soldiers on July 1, 2, 3, 1863, has become a place for solemn contemplation of the greatest question of all:

Is there life after death?

While only a relatively few humans experienced the Battle of Gettysburg firsthand, *all* of us, throughout all of history and all of the future, have and will experience death.

In the past, Gettysburg was a place for predominantly male, military-historian mindsets, where one studied three short days in all of Time. Now, everyone can visit with an eye to the Eternities.

Gettysburg has finally become what Major General Joshua Chamberlain, who fought at Gettysburg, envisioned when he spoke there in 1889. "On great fields something stays. Forms change and pass; bodies disappear; but spirits linger, to consecrate ground . . ." It has become, as he foresaw, a "deathless field." Gettysburg has come to be, as he predicted, "the vision-place of souls."

*   *   *

Gettysburg is well known for its paranormal activity, and for good reason. More people died young and suddenly, under tragic circumstances, at a high level of emotion, than anywhere else in the entire United States. Fifty-one thousand casualties in three days of battle. Actually, the casualty rate was more astounding than that, since the soldiers fought only about twenty-four hours out of the three days. Fifty-one thousand men killed or wounded in twenty-four hours means that for every hour they fought, 2,125 men were shot. Every minute of those twenty-four hours, almost 36 men were hit by flying metal. Every two seconds, a man was hit. *For twenty-four hours.*

Many of the wounded were not cared for right away, and suffered for days under the hot sun, then the pouring rain, out in the very fields where visitors tread today. Most died in physical agony; and nearly all died in mental agony, thinking of those loved ones they would leave behind. Hospital sites were areas of particular emotional travail as hundreds were clustered together, hoping to survive to see their families again.

Some started to get better, their hopes of getting home rising until dashed to pieces by the cruel happenstance of the era in which they fought. Because antiseptics were unknown at the time, a man with a minor wound would have it treated by a doctor who had just explored an abdominal wound, thus unknowingly introducing deadly bacteria into the bloodstream. The patient would be doing fine for about two weeks, then infection would set in and kill the unbelieving soldier within hours.

Bodies of soldiers slain on the field of battle were dragged together and buried where they had fought and died. Some officers received special treatment and were identified. The common soldier was identified if possible; more likely he was buried hastily in an unmarked grave in hopes that someone would later be able to identify him. Mass graves were often utilized when the stench of decomposing bodies became a problem. Hardly any had the benefit of a sanctified burial.

Virtually every man who died at Gettysburg was buried at least twice: once where they fought and died on the field and then in an official cemetery. The Union soldiers were gathered and taken to the new National Cemetery, which was dedicated and consecrated on November 19, 1863. Confederates lay buried on the battlefield until the early 1870's, when families in the former Confederacy requested the bodies of their relatives be exhumed and sent south. Local Gettysburg contractors were procured for the duty. Needless to say, after seven years, un-embalmed, in the Pennsylvania soil, there was not much left of loved ones to identify and send home.

Sadly, most historians agree that between 800 and 1,500 were never found and must still lie, un-sanctified, out in the fields where they struggled, hoped, prayed, suffered, died and were buried nearly a century-and-a-half ago.

If there ever was a place ripe for perturbed spirits to roam for Eternity, it is Gettysburg.

*   *   *

"Where can we find ghosts at Gettysburg?" It is one of the most common questions asked by visitors to the *Ghosts of Gettysburg Candlelight Walking Tours*® Headquarters.

Unfortunately, the ghosts do not hand out a schedule, like park rangers, to tell us when they are going to appear and give a talk.

However, there seem to be places in the town, on the battlefield, and even as far away as neighboring towns, where paranormal activity occurs more frequently. As well, there seem to be certain times and seasons—even years—when the unexplainable activity happens more often.

While I cannot give you a specific time or place where you may intercept the spirits on their journeys around the area made infamous by the slaughter between thousands of countrymen, I *can* give you advice on the techniques, equipment, times of day, month or year, and probable locations to help in your quest to encounter one of the Ghosts of Gettysburg.

WHAT IS A GHOST?

According to Rosemary Ellen Guiley in her *Encyclopedia of Ghosts and Spirits*, quite simply, a ghost is an alleged spirit of the dead. The age-old definition is that a ghost is a disembodied soul, which, after the life of its body is over, goes on to live an existence apart from the visible world. Renowned ghost hunter Hans Holzer's definition adds a more sinister twist: "ghosts are the surviving mental faculties of people who died traumatically."[1] This would seem to apply to just about every soldier who died at Gettysburg.

Numerous parapsychologists have gone on to attempt to classify various *types* of ghosts according to their activities and manifestations.

Joshua P. Warren, in *How to Hunt Ghosts*, classifies ghosts into five general categories: Entities, Imprints, Warps, Poltergeists, and Naturals, and in so doing helps to explain why so many paranormal experiences seem so different.

An Entity, according to Warren, appears to have a consciousness and interacts with the observer. Entities can come from the past—the ones we most expect to see at Gettysburg—but can also appear from the present, as in living humans projecting their own spirit to another site.[2] As well, Entities can come from the future, as harbingers of good or ominous news. Entities, Warren writes, may use the natural electrical environment to appear and "can create objective and subjective experiences."

The very first ghost story of Gettysburg comes from the soldiers, themselves, seeing an Entity from the past.

Through the misty night, during the forced march to Gettysburg, the men of the Union Army's Fifth Corps see a horseman riding before their column. He rides ahead, seemingly leading the way, then waits for the men to catch up. Some think they can barely make out the figure, who seems to be dressed in a tri-corn hat and cape, the uniform of a previous war. As they get closer, a weird rumor floats back along the column: the men have seen him and have seen the impossible. It is General George Washington, dead now some 63 years, leading the army of the United States once again, from the Beyond. It is a portent, the exhausted men believe, of certain victory, of help from Heaven to save the Union.

Imprints may also appear frequently at Gettysburg. An Imprint can appear as a place (altered into its original, past appearance) or any once-existing person, animal or thing. These ghosts do not interact with the living and often appear unconscious of their surroundings. The same scene may be played over and over, like the numerous sightings of the "Phantom Regiment" at Gettysburg, drilling and drilling and drilling, marching again into the now defunct battle like robots.

The dignitaries on Little Round Top all agreed how thoughtful and impressive it was for the National Park Service to arrange for the Civil War reenactors to demonstrate the drilling of a battalion in the famed Valley of Death below them. The unit wheeled and halted, went through the manual of arms, then marched off to disappear into the woods nearby. The dignitaries were not told it was going to happen, and so it was a delightful surprise. The ranger in charge was surprised too, when they thanked him effusively for the demonstration, for the Park Service had arranged no such thing, nor were there any reenactment groups, over which the Park Service exercises strict control, visiting the park that day. It was not the last time it happened either . . .[3]

I have often referred to this as a residual haunting, created when the emotions (given off as electrical pulses) are so strong as to remain embedded in the surrounding environment then released under certain conditions. If the paranormal occurrences persist through more than one "group" of observers, the site can be classified as "haunted."

Warps appear to be a brief vision into another time or dimension, like the horrifying hospital scene in the basement suddenly—and reluctantly— witnessed from the elevator of Pennsylvania Hall at Gettysburg College.[4] In the case of Warps, the location has much to do with the ghostly activity. At Gettysburg, the geology or the materials used in the construction of buildings seem to have a lot to do with "Warps." Warren identifies the Warp as one of the "most complicated issues facing science today," since within these places, the laws of physics seem to disappear, time seems altered, logic is turned upside down, and numerous paranormal activities can be experienced.

Poltergeist activity ("poltergeist" is German for "noisy ghost") probably occurs because of human mental activity. It has most often been associated with adolescents and telekinesis, the use of the mind to move physical objects. A large number of activities recorded at Gettysburg College, such as objects levitating from shelves, doors slamming, or lights turning on and off, may be the result of the living beings' high emotional state, producing poltergeist activity.[5]

What Warren calls Naturals are unusual phenomena that have many of the earmarks of a ghost, but are actually caused by explainable (or eventually explainable) science.[6] Examples of this type of phenomena have been sighted at Gettysburg as well.

An account recorded by the Civilian Conservation Corps in the 1930's given by a man who had worked out at the Rose Farm in the few weeks after the battle recalls an odd sighting. Returning after dark, past the fresh mounds of earth covering the tons of putrefying human gore, the man claimed to have seen a glow, a phosphorescent light hovering over the unquiet resting-place of perturbed spirits. Swamp-gas, some might say today; ectoplasm ascending, without a doubt, say others . . .

Troy Taylor, in *The Ghost Hunter's Guidebook*, classifies ghosts generally in the same manner, but with different names.

There are Intelligent Hauntings, where the ghost will interact with living beings, similar to an Entity; a Residual Haunting, in which there is no "intelligence" to the spirit and where the spirit is apparently linked to the location, like the "Phantom Regiment;" Poltergeist Activity; and Portal Hauntings, which coincide with a vision into the past, or some sort of veil being parted, for a paranormal event to be witnessed.

To these, Taylor adds several other types of ghostly events.

There is the Crises Apparition, which is allegedly the spirit of one who has just died and appears to a member of the family or a friend to bid them good-bye.

There are Ghost Lights, which, according to Taylor, may be attributed to a natural phenomena and may or may not have anything to with the spirits of the dead. There are numerous accounts of "ghost lights" at Gettysburg. In addition to the scores of campfires in the South Mountains on the anniversary of the Confederates' presence, there are the candle lanterns moving weirdly through the fields of great slaughter, such as the Valley of Death, and campfires in the Wheatfield, which do not seem to be associated with any "natural" phenomena by the way they act or by the inconsistency with which they appear.

Taylor cites one more type of spirit: the "Man-Made Ghost," wherein researchers "invented" a ghost, and called upon him to manifest himself—which he did! Taylor, however, acknowledged the possibility that this may have been more like a poltergeist than a true spirit coming forth.

Psychic Pam Saylor once listed five reasons why spirits linger at the place where they left their mortal bodies: 1) An abrupt death; 2) A person's belief system; 3) Concern for those left behind; 4) To contact the living to give a message of hope; 5) The living are grieving too long for a loved one and the loved one cannot move on.

Later she added a more ominous reason: A fear of final judgement.

Death in the Battle of Gettysburg was nearly always abrupt. Men atomized by exploding artillery or blown apart by canister or knocked brain-dead by an ounce of lead to the head, die abruptly. Sometimes, if we concede that consciousness continues after death, they did not acknowledge, or even realize, they were dead. If they were wounded, nearly universally their first thoughts were of their loved ones left behind. In an era of spiritualism and religious revivals, they all knew on some level, that they were committing the mortal sin of killing their fellow man and must, sooner or later, face their Maker to account for it. Fifty-one thousand men, suddenly thrown into death or the contemplation of death. And we come today—about 1.6 million of us every year—to commemorate their deaths, to mourn them as we have done for nearly a century-and-a-half, grieving for them far too long.

If ever there was a place made and nurtured just for the existence of ghosts . . . it is Gettysburg . . .

*   *   *

There has long been a debate as to whether there is *any* kind of existence after death. Yet science proves that human-like creatures have believed in some sort of life after death for nearly all of our history. Every major religion on the face of the earth propounds an existence that transcends this one.

According to the Smithsonian Institution, there is archeological evidence that Neanderthals buried their dead with tools, weapons, and food 70,000 years ago, an indication that they believed these things were needed after death.

There is also evidence that many ancient cultures did the same for the deceased. The most famous of these, of course, was the Egyptian, which mummified their dead and buried them with their possessions for the Next World. One must wonder what it was that convinced these ancient people that those who died needed sustenance post-mortem. Did one (or many) of them appear after death to convince the living that some sort of life went on beyond the grave?

Aristotle was the first famous individual to actually deny the existence of life after death, claiming that since conscious thought comes from the biological matter of the brain, when the brain dies so does all existence. Death, to him, was the total destruction of personality.

Yet another great philosopher, René Descartes argued that the physical body and the "mind" are separate, and destruction of the brain does not necessarily mean obliteration of "mind."

High priests of numerous Eastern religions pride themselves on their ability to separate body and mind, and to be able to reach a different plane of consciousness, leaving their mortal forms of flesh and blood behind.

Countless modern studies of people who have "died" and been revived, record them bringing back eerily similar descriptions of the experiences they had while "dead."[7] Men and women have described floating above their bodies, looking down, and seeing themselves after falling into unconsciousness because their heart and breathing have stopped. Almost universally they see a long tunnel of light and previously deceased relatives in this new realm. Usually

14

one will escort them back to their body and explain that it is not yet their time, whereupon they will awaken, resuscitated.

Some scientists explain this as only an hallucination of the dying brain, when neurons are still firing and thoughts are still being created. But there are accounts of people who have "flat-lined"—have no brain activity at all—undergoing surgery, who have had the same experiences.[8]

More recently, others have postulated that consciousness does not exist solely in the individual brain, but all around us in a "field" of subtle energy.[9] All consciousness resonates through this field, which may explain many paranormal events, such as pre-cognition (seeing into the future), psychic readings of historic structures or events, ghosts and ghostly activity.

Although mankind has invented countless ways of sending an individual *into* the world of death, a successful way of bringing one back is, as they say, still on the drawing table. Volunteers for the ultimate journey and dubious return, understandably, are few and far between. So we must gather data from observation, the time-honored method of doing science for millennia before the "scientific method" was introduced in relatively recent times.

Let us analyze, then, what we know, starting off by eliminating the fiction propagated by storytellers, horror novelists, and Hollywood.

With few exceptions, ghosts have been relegated to the horror genre of films and novels, or the "urban legends" of late night slumber parties or campfire gatherings. An encounter with a "ghost," via Hollywood, pulp fiction, or the best storyteller at the campfire, is something to be avoided—if you can—because the ghost entity is able to maim, kill, and mutilate your body, or, worse yet, steal your soul and inhabit what is left of your mortal form.

Or some more hideous variations of that theme.

At least according to the observations collected in recent books about paranormal events, these popular sources for ghost lore contain numerous common misconceptions, not the least of which is the aggressive aspect of ghosts.

After collecting well over 600 stories, and consulting with numerous other ghost story collectors and authors, a malevolent spirit seems the most rare of all creatures. I have encountered only two that perpetrated physical harm upon a human.

Dr. Charles Emmons, in his cross-cultural book *Chinese Ghosts and ESP*, found, after analyzing over 300 stories of hauntings, that the Chinese believe that ghosts are actually dead relatives who return to an individual to chastise them for bad behavior.

Because of Hollywood, many people think that ghosts only come out at night, yet at least 40–45 percent of all the stories in my books have occurred during the daylight hours.

Others believe that ghosts look like people under bed sheets, or like Casper, the Friendly Ghost (implying, of course, that all others are not amiable). From my experience, virtually all of the Hollywood stereotypes are misleading.

*   *   *

In order to "hunt" ghosts, one must first know what one is looking for. How do ghosts manifest themselves? How do you know when you are in the presence of one of the Ghosts of Gettysburg?

One of the most common questions people get when discussing the paranormal with others is, "Have you ever seen a ghost?" Compelled by honesty, most people have to answer, "no."

That, however, does not mean they have not had a paranormal experience or encountered a ghost.

Virtually all the senses are involved in paranormal happenings: hearing, smelling, touching, feeling, as well as seeing. According to statistics extrapolated from the over 600 stories I have collected, and from other works, only about 10–11 percent of all paranormal experiences are visual. By far, the most common paranormal experiences (about 60 percent) are auditory. In other words, you will hear a ghost before you will see one.

But be aware that all of the human senses are susceptible to paranormal stimuli, including that intangible "feeling" one gets upon occasion.

I liken it to the times when you are sitting with your back toward the door. Suddenly, you get the feeling that you are being watched. You turn around and, unbeknownst to you, your wife or child or a friend has silently stood at the doorway watching you. You had no clue they were there, but you "felt" it enough to actually turn and look.

Author Rupert Sheldrake attributes this very real phenomenon to a "perceptual field" that is apparently linked to the activity of the brain. The field "stretches out far beyond the body [of the viewer] to embrace whatever is being perceived."[10]

But another time, you will be sitting with your back toward the door and get that same feeling—someone is watching you. You turn around, expecting to see someone familiar at the doorway and . . .*nobody is there*! Same feeling, same positive knowledge that someone is right behind you, except that there is no one. Or, at least, no one visible. *Someone* must have been there, you are convinced, since you had exactly the same feeling and were compelled to do the same action—turn and greet them.

Perhaps "someone" *was* there, someone who still possesses the energy to create that perceptual field; one who is dead, but still exists in spirit form.

The important thing is, do not deny your feelings. We, as children, may once have been much more sensitive to psychic phenomena, but kind-hearted,

16

practical parents told us time and time again, "There's no one in the room with you when we turn out your lights," or "Those are just imaginary friends you talk about seeing: they don't really exist." Our psychic sensitivity was drummed out of us by a realistic world—a world that may be denying the ultimate reality simply because it cannot face it. Here is your chance to regain your psychic sensitivities. Do not deny what you feel. As more than one "professional" ghost investigator has said, *you* are probably the best, most sensitive ghost detecting instrument available.

Through what other human senses will ghosts manifest themselves?

Time and time again members of the *Ghosts of Gettysburg* tour groups will smell tobacco smoke. Interestingly enough, one person will smell the pungent odor of a pipe, while someone standing right next to them will not. As we all know from experience, when someone lights up tobacco products, it is just a moment or two before the smell permeates the area and everyone can smell it. The fact that one person can smell the tobacco and another standing right next to them cannot, indicates that it is a paranormal event: each person is reacting according to their own individual psychic sensitivity.

Others, in areas where the battle raged fiercely, have smelled the rotten-egg smell of black powder—fourteen decades after the last musket or cannon shot was fired. Still others will get a ghastly whiff of rotting meat—the ubiquitous odor that permeated the battlefield—nearly a century-and-a-half after the last decomposing corpse was removed and buried.

How else can ghosts be detected?

Joshua Warren experimented with electrical charges blowing as an "ion wind" across the skin of a subject. They reported that it felt cold, as though someone touched them. We know that, according to electromagnetic field meters, paranormal anomalies register an electrical charge. Could it be this electrical charge that "tapped" a young female student on the shoulder as she moved into a well-documented haunted house on Carlisle Street in Gettysburg?[11] Could an "ion wind" produced by entities be the source of repeated reports of people getting a chill just before they encounter a ghost?

As I previously stated, seeing a ghost is relatively rare, and when seen, their appearance is often more confusing than frightening.

"Orbs" are the most common thing that people identify—or confuse—with ghosts. Literally hundreds of photos of orbs are brought or mailed to the *Ghosts of Gettysburg Candlelight Walking Tours*® Headquarters. Many are legitimate anomalies captured on film or digital memory cards. However, orbs are the easiest phenomenon to fake or mistake.

Orbs appear as translucent balls of light, often with concentric rings and what appears to be a nucleus. Warren writes that phantoms travel in the shape of an orb because it is the "most energy-efficient." Like water suspended in air, they take the form of their "container."

Orbs in the Attic of Ghosts of Gettysburg Headquarters

Dust, mist, rain, snow, hair, lint, and certain insects, if close enough to the lens of an automatic-focus camera (which is already focusing on something in the distance) can all appear as orbs. Sometimes the only way to be sure the orb you have captured on film is a spirit, is to eliminate all the other possibilities. This is why documenting the investigative session, either on paper or by recording it with a video camera, is so important. Keep all the details associated with the investigation—time, temperature, relative humidity, weather conditions—so that bogus causes which produce orbs can be ruled out. There are times when you can be pretty much assured that what you have captured is a true anomaly. Orbs that appear partially behind something which is at a distance—such as a tree or fence-post—can obviously not be anything too close to the lens to be out-of-focus.

Orbs that appear in videos, moving slowly or suddenly tearing away at impossible speeds, or even, as in one case at Herr Tavern in Gettysburg, doing a little dance in front of the video camera at the request of the investigator, are readily identifiable as anomalies and virtually impossible to fake.[12]

Orbs seen with the naked eye are obviously not faked. My own experience is illustrative.

Rick Fisher, Director of the Pennsylvania Paranormal Society, had taken me out to Sachs Covered Bridge for an investigation. At this point, even though I had written two books on ghosts at Gettysburg, I was still an extreme skeptic, especially where orbs were involved. I was sure they were simply pieces of dust, casually drifting in front of the camera lens which was focused upon something in the distance. As we stood at the end of the bridge nearest the parking area, he handed me his night vision scope and said, "I want you to look down the length of the bridge."

I stood with my eye pressed to the eyepiece for at least a minute. Nothing happened. "What am I looking for?" I asked Rick. "You'll know when you see it," he said confidently.

Within a few more seconds I was again becoming bored. Suddenly, I saw it.

A huge ball of light came through—*through*—the roof of the bridge, paused briefly before my face, did a 90 degree turn to the left, and flashed at an incalculable speed out through the side of the bridge. As the saying goes, you could have knocked me over with a feather.

I no doubt issued an explicative at which Rick laughed, then smiled knowingly.

From that moment I knew that orbs were something completely different from anything else I had ever encountered.

In another instance, a fellow investigator watched an orb come *through* the windshield of my van, float between us and move to the back of the van. She took a picture. There in the back of the van was the orb, suspended near the back door.

Paranormal mists are another way entities manifest themselves. Paranormal investigators once referred to these mists as "ectoplasm," an archaic term associated with 19th Century spiritualists who often faked sessions using fabricated "ectoplasm" emanating from their mouths, noses, and other orifices. To avoid the stigma of fakery, paranormal mist is a better term for the ropey, swirling, smoky clouds that are often photographed in allegedly haunted places, or sometimes seen by the naked eye.

At Gettysburg, on certain nights, there will lay along the ground where men were once mowed down in straight lines, clouds of thick mist. It is quite a shock to be driving along the Emmitsburg Road, on a clear, starlit night, then suddenly be blinded by a seemingly impenetrable fog. Yet, as quickly as you are in it, you are again out of it, because it is only as thick as a double-ranked line of infantry of the Civil War era . . .

Joshua Warren attributes the ability to see a ghost to plasma (not to be confused with "ectoplasm," the phoney spiritualists' tool). Plasma is, in addition to solids, liquids, and gasses, a fourth state of matter. An electrical spark is plasma. It represents a change in the state of matter as energy moves from one point to another "showing" us electricity, which is normally invisible energy. Warren theorizes that, since ghosts contain electrical or electromagnetic energy (as evidenced by electromagnetic field meters), a charged plasma, in the form of a mist (and perhaps an orb) is one way they can be seen. The spirit-energy of the dead may use the electrical charge to arrange charged particles in the surrounding atmosphere to make itself visible, like iron filings make the energy of a magnet visible.

Paranormal Mist at Sachs Bridge

It may be plasma that shows up in photos identified as having captured "vortexes." A vortex is a solid white mass that seems to be swirling before the lens. It may be a stage in the evolution of a ghost: from orb to paranormal mist to vortex. Or it may be a type of energy all its own, forming itself into a column. Vortexes are one of the most common manifestations of energy in nature, from high and low pressure areas in meteorology to hurricanes and tornadoes, to simple whirlpools in a sink when the plug is pulled. Why wouldn't paranormal energy also take such a natural form as a vortex?

Courtesy of David Livingston
Photo of a Vortex

Photos taken in and around Gettysburg have also shown strange pencil-thin streaks of light "dancing" through the shot. Sometimes small orbs can be seen strung together within the streak, giving it a rope-like appearance. The streaks range in color from yellow and white to green and red.

I have been shown photos, taken on the darkened battlefield, that looked like a picture of red and orange flames leaping before the camera. The frames were in the middle of the roll of 35mm film, negating the possibility that the film had been exposed when the camera was loaded or unloaded. I asked if perhaps the film was faulty. But the photos were taken at two separate times with two different rolls of film.

CAUTION! A camera strap hanging in front of the lens or a finger inadvertently photographed "close-up" can be mistaken for a vortex. Remove camera straps before any investigation. Always extinguish smoking materials since tobacco smoke produces clouds that photograph like paranormal mist. During cold-weather investigations, hold your breath while photographing. Use a tripod and step back from video equipment whenever you can. Photographing during mist, rain, snow or dusty conditions also produces bogus orbs. Note and record weather conditions for all investigations.

Most commonly, Ghosts at Gettysburg can be heard. Echoing down time in numerous, ancient houses in Gettysburg are phantom footsteps moving across the floor above one's head, or down a flight of stairs; from the darkened woods on the battlefield, desperate shouts of men in combat who fought and died a century-and-a-half ago; wafting across a wind-swept valley, the roar of cannons or musketry long silenced by time. Often, these sounds can be captured on digital or analog tape recorders. Researchers have named the unheard noise, with no apparent source, which is captured on audio devices, "E. V. P." or Electronic Voice Phenomena. It is one of the most bizarre, unbelievable, yet tangible manifestations of ghosts at Gettysburg and will be discussed in a following chapter.

WHY GHOSTS EXIST AT GETTYSBURG

Gettysburg, before July 1, 1863, was just a small cross-roads town in south-central Pennsylvania. After July 1, 1863, it would be recognized as the site of the bloodiest battle ever fought on the North American Continent and one of the bloodiest and most decisive battles in all of world history.

Because of the vast interest in understanding the battle, much research has already been done and published. That research can be used to assist paranormal investigators in finding places on the battlefield or in the town of Gettysburg which are more likely to yield paranormal activity . . . or to help them stir it up!

The Gettysburg Campaign—the movements of the Union and Confederate Armies to Gettysburg—began in the first week of June, 1863, when Robert E. Lee marched his Confederate Army of Northern Virginia into the Shenandoah Valley and headed north.

As Lee's army moved north, the Union Army was ordered to stay between the invaders and Washington, the capital of the Northern States.

There were several engagements fought between elements of the two armies as they maneuvered through Virginia, Maryland, and Pennsylvania; small battles that left men just as cold and dead as the climactic Battle of Gettysburg. The route to Gettysburg is strewn with gravesites—both known and unknown—alongside major highways and dirt farm lanes and in innumerable private family cemeteries. We may never know the number of poor soldiers who, in the heat wave of mid-June, 1863, just lay down at the side of the road and died from heatstroke. Those poor souls were buried, no doubt, by some beneficent stranger in an unmarked and forgotten grave nearby.[1]

By the end of June, elements of the Confederate Army were near the Susquehanna River to the east and north of Gettysburg, threatening Harrisburg, the capital of Pennsylvania. They were also west of Gettysburg, in Chambersburg and Cashtown.

A former owner of the Cashtown Inn suggested that through his front door passed more Confederate officers than any other door in America. He was probably right, since Robert E. Lee used the building as a temporary headquarters and much of the Confederate army passed through Cashtown. All of Lee's subordinates would have checked in with their commander, passing in and out of that very door, making decisions that would change the course of both world history and the personal histories of some 175,000 men and boys . . .

On the night of June 30, 1863, a couple of thousand Union cavalrymen bivouacked on the western outskirts of Gettysburg, along McPherson's Ridge, never realizing that for some, it would be their last sleep upon this earth.

Early in the morning of July 1, 1863, Confederate infantry, marching eastward along the Cashtown to Gettysburg Pike, clashed with those Union cavalrymen. The battle lasted for a couple of hours, until Union Major General John F. Reynolds led his First Corps infantrymen into line to replace the exhausted cavalrymen. He was turning in the saddle to watch his troops approach when he was shot in the back of the neck and fell, dying, from his horse, becoming the highest ranking Union officer to perish in the battle. A professional soldier, he was a participant in the greatest battle of his generation for less than half an hour.

The woods southeast of the McPherson Barn would come to be known as "Reynolds' Woods" and, as some have witnessed, one of the more supernaturally active places on the battlefield. More on that later . . .

The fighting on the first day escalated as more troops arrived on the battlefield. The lines stretched in a north/south orientation, from the Lutheran Theological Seminary north to Oak Hill, where the Peace Light now stands. From there they bent back to the right and formed an east/west leg that extended to Barlow's Knoll and the Harrisburg Road.

From the moment the fighting started, wounded men were evacuated to the larger buildings behind the battle lines: Old Dorm and Krauth House at the Lutheran Seminary, and Pennsylvania Hall on the college campus. Behind the Confederate lines, a large wooded lot would become the site for numerous hospitals for wounded Southerners and receive the name "Hospital Woods" because of it. Churches in Gettysburg and the courthouse became jammed with wounded, mutilated, dying men. Amputations began immediately, as did the screams from the wretched patients. The public buildings began to overflow into the private houses in town. Before long, sections of the seminary and college campuses became graveyards, as did the yards and kitchen gardens of the townspeople.

The places where humans have suffered greatly are often the sticking-place of their souls after they have died. Some spirits are even said to return, after having escaped, to the place where the body suffered immensely, even though they may have died decades later and miles away. Somehow, for whatever reason, they return, leave and return again to the place of their past personal horror . . .

In the afternoon the Union line imploded upon itself and thousands of panicked, desperate Union soldiers streamed back into the town, chased by Confederates. They ran through the fields around the town and through the college. Down the streets and alleys of Gettysburg they tumbled, and up the long slope to an elevation ominously named Cemetery Hill. Dusk brought an end to the fighting.

It is a scientific fact that humans generate large amounts of electrical energy, especially when under stress or on an emotional "high," or even when they are merely thinking. Paranormalists theorize that, this electrical energy can be transmitted—like electromagnetic waves—and embed itself into the rock or brick or wood that is used for construction materials in structures. This energy is, under the right conditions, released, and accounts for human-like noises, apparitions, and electrostatic "feelings" like the hair on the back of one's neck rising when in an ancient building . . .

Night brought more troops to the fields and ridges outside the small town. Union forces, as they were brought up, extended down the ridge that ran south from the cemetery on the hill, and spread to the next hill over, Culp's Hill, named after the local family that owned most of it. The line formed the shape of a giant fishhook.

The arriving Confederate Army outlined that hook and took positions east of Cemetery Hill, occupied the town of Gettysburg itself, and stretched down the ridge that extended southward from the Lutheran Seminary.

During the afternoon and evening of July 2, Lee attacked both ends of the Union fishhook-shaped line. Fighting raged through the Peach Orchard on the Emmitsburg Road, stained the crops in the Wheatfield crimson, ripped boys apart in an oddly-shaped Triangular Field, left blood pooled on the rocks at Devil's Den, and wasted lives like they were less than nothing on the slopes of Little Round Top.

Little Round Top

Later, men would die long into the darkness in attacks upon East Cemetery and Culp's Hills. Those who did not die would echo their fading cries for help through the eerie darkness of a place they may have never even heard the name of: *Gettysburg*.

Though the fighting on the third day at Gettysburg seems to attract the most attention for its gory conclusion, the fighting on the second day—July 2, 1863—no doubt was the bloodiest in the three-day battle. Most of the 51,000 casualties occurred on that day and were spread all over the battlefield. The suffering and dying was pandemic . . .

On July 3, Lee set in motion the plan for Pickett's Charge, a name now synonymous with defeat and devastation. Of the 12,500 Confederate troops that began the charge, two-thirds became casualties across the broad, open plain between Cemetery and Seminary Ridges.

Field of Pickett's Charge

One cannot imagine a more emotion-laden event than a grand charge on an enemy's battle lines. Not only were men concerned with the life or death of their country and the imminent death of dear friends who marched next to them into battle, but with their own, personal extinction as well. The thought that you could be horribly wounded, or sent on the one-way trip to the strange Other World, or to oblivion, or to meet, face-to-face, your God or Satan—in the next twenty minutes—brings your emotions to a pitch and focus greater than you have ever known before. Multiply this by 12,500 and you cannot calculate the amount of emotional energy thrown off before the Confederate assault upon the Union lines on July 3, 1863, at Gettysburg . . .

The next day—Independence Day—the two armies sat and watched each other through a pouring rain. The survivors of the battle, looking in the drizzling night like ghouls, searched for fallen comrades. That night and in the early morning hours of July 5, Robert E. Lee took his battered Army of Northern Virginia back toward Virginia with a wagon train of wounded stretching 17 miles in length.

The entire 3-day battle would claim from 44,000 to 51,000 casualties—killed, wounded, and missing. Many of the missing reflect those so badly mutilated by artillery fire that they could not be recognized.

The dead were gathered and buried in shallow graves generally where they fell on the battlefield—in orchards, fields, pastures, in dooryard gardens next to farmhouses. The bodies were identified sometimes by friends, more often by letters in their pockets or state belt-buckles or buttons, since official government-issued "dog tags" were not in use. Often they were not identified at all, especially in the case of the Confederates, since they were the attacking force and left their dead in the hands of the enemy when they retreated.

Within a few months the locals began to complain to state officials: the decomposing dead were being exposed by the weather and roaming animals; the stench was horrific, the sight of rotting bodies even worse. A National Cemetery for the heroic dead was proposed and established on Cemetery Hill and the exhumation and reburial of the dead was started.

But only the Union dead.

The Confederates, being considered the enemy, were left in their shallow graves to be tended by local good-Samaritans. Their bodies would eventually be exhumed and shipped home, but not until the early 1870's. By then there was little left of the Confederate heroes, and several men would fit in one shipping box. It was a sad end for Americans from the southern states who believed in their cause and country just as fervently as the Americans from the North.

Still, all have not yet found peace at Gettysburg. As recently as a few years ago, bodies—or actually just bones wrapped in the tattered remnants of a uniform—were found and re-buried with much ceremony in the National Cemetery.

Nearly every religion agrees that there must be some sort of consecration, some kind of sanctification of ground, some blessing, for the soul to rest peacefully as the body is buried. This is not just to calm the living. It is common consensus in all the major religions, written down as Holy Rites, that it is the deceased's soul that is in danger without the proper burial observance. "Hallowing" ground for the receiving of the deceased, some believe, assures that the dead will rest in peace; without benediction, some believe, the soul is left to wander forever . . .

With so many souls gone to their Maker within a few days inside such small areas as encompass the Wheatfield, or Little Round Top, or the deadly field of Pickett's Charge, it is no wonder that spectral sightings and paranormal whisperings are still heard on the great battlefield of Gettysburg.

GETTYSBURG: THE PARANORMAL EXPERIENCE

Analysis of the vast number of stories that I have collected, along with numerous investigations at allegedly haunted sites in and around Gettysburg, has amassed a great deal of data. Before attempting to classify anything, let us first look at the information collected. Since the word "ghosts" already pre-supposes an established set of data, for now, think of what we are studying as merely "subjects."

Here's what we know about the "subjects" at Gettysburg:

—The subjects may represent some sort of heat energy because they give off cold (and sometimes heat) that can be felt by persons coming in contact with, or near, them. We also know this from the use of proximity thermometers ("thermal scanners"), so it is not just a person's imagination. Dr. Charles Emmons has pointed out that it is important that a person feels cold *before* experiencing the paranormal, since *after* a frightening experience, the small blood vessels close down and that is why we feel a chill.

It was during an investigation with Rick Fisher that I was attracting orbs—the photos taken show them, one-by-one, closing in on me. As I stood there, the chill began to permeate my body; my hands grew so stiff that I could not make a fist. I had to walk away from the spot. As I did, it was like walking into an oven, relatively speaking. I was warm again, once I got away from those elusive orbs, which I could not see, but were showing up on all the photos . . .

—The subjects appear to reflect light (a camera flash) and so must have some substance to them that can sometimes be seen by the naked eye, but more often in photographs. They may even generate their own light energy, or possibly be stimulated into glowing (like bio-luminescence in certain marine creatures) by a camera flash or infrared lights.

—Our subjects sometimes appear white, with a bluish core and tint; other colors, particularly red, red-orange, and gold are seen. Occasionally even the rainbow spectrum is seen.

A couple showed me a panoramic photo they had taken of the Triangular Field. In it was what looked like a statue, and they asked if I noticed anything unusual about it. Of course, I said there was no statue in the Triangular Field. They agreed and showed me an enlargement of the anomaly. It appeared to be the form of a man, bent over as if advancing with a musket. The remarkable thing was that the image held all the colors of the rainbow....[1]

—The subjects are in motion; they even rise–something cold air does not do. They have been videotaped moving toward, away from, and perpendicular to the camera's viewpoint.

After an investigation at East Cavalry Battlefield, my fellow investigator and I began walking back to my van. My video camera was on a tripod—I always videotape my investigations so that no one can say anything was "faked"—and as we approached the camera, suddenly several orbs, as if they were flying away from us, rushed at the camera lens, only to veer away at the last second, as if they had some sort of intelligence to them . . .

—The subjects have electromagnetic properties. Gauss meters—electromagnetic detectors—spike when in the presence of an "orb" or "paranormal mist." The subjects also drain electricity from batteries, or activate or deactivate the electronics in cameras. Perhaps one way they communicate is through electromagnetism, since magnetic tape and digital recorders capture their sounds when they cannot be heard with the human ear. Which leads us to one of my pet theories: If sensitive, man-made, electromagnetic devices can be affected by orbs or paranormal mist, why not biological electromagnetically sensitive areas such as the optic or auditory nerves, or the right temporal lobe area of the brain. Perhaps these "subjects" communicate by direct electromagnetic sensory interface, interposing their energy between the synapses of our optic, auditory, tactile, and olfactory nerve systems or directly into the area of the brain most associated with paranormal experiences—the mesial right temporal lobe.[2] This may explain why the majority of paranormal "subjects" appear as partially-developed images, or why their auditory expressions are not always articulate.

In the "Ghost Photo Gallery" in the Ghosts of Gettysburg Tour Headquarters there is a picture of a young investigator, an electromagnetic field detector in his hand, eyes wide after hearing it go off. In the photo is an orb, no doubt the reason the EMF detector spiked . . .

—The subjects are able to "gather" about a person as shown in photos taken moments apart. Some feel this is a sign of curiosity, an animal (and human) trait.

—The subjects appear to move intelligently, responding to specific requests. They respond intelligently, through E.V.P., to specific questions.

There was the investigator at Herr Tavern who requested that, if there were any spirits in the room, they show themselves. On the video tape, you can watch as an orb moves to the front of the lens, darts about in a little dance to "show" itself, then, as if suddenly aware of what it did, zooms away . . .

—They often change shape, going from "orb" form to misty, ropey, cloudy shapes, to full human body (or body part) shapes.

I was returning home down the alley behind my house on Carlisle Street, a part of the battlefield. As my headlights reached to the end of the alley, I saw a small, cloudy mist near the ground. "Is that a dog?" I heard myself ask. "No, too big. A deer? No, too tall." By then it had grown to nearly six feet tall. "A prowler," was my final guess as the shape it had taken suddenly reminded me of the height and width of a human . . .

Now, think about our classic definition of a "ghost": They are white and change shape; they sometimes communicate, like Hamlet's Father's ghost; they make the hair stand up on your body, perhaps from the cold, but that also happens with electromagnetic or static electricity; they move and sometimes follow us as if curious; they will sometimes respond to us by moving, or moving other objects; seemingly for no reason they alter their appearance, or appear and, just as mysteriously, disappear.

Therefore, the raw data we have collected on our "subjects" at Gettysburg seems to match what past generations of observers have seen and named "ghosts."

Yet some researchers feel that as many as 98 percent of all reports of ghosts have normal explanations, including scientific phenomena—such as methane gas, tricks of light, electrical charges in the air—as well as psychological phenomena, like dreams and hallucinations.

For example, Thomas Carson, a Gettysburgian visiting the area of Big Round Top after the battle, saw a strange phenomena he may have attributed to the shucking off of souls after death. Remaining in the vicinity of a number of shallow graves until after sunset, he witnessed a singular phosphorescence emanating from the ground over the burials. It is unknown whether Carson knew about methane gas. It is also unknown how much longer after dark he remained in the area.[3] There is at least one other account of a glowing, rising substance coming from graves after the battle.

*   *   *

There is disagreement among researchers as to whether the "ghost" is a true, objective, physical manifestation apart from the observer, or a projection—be it visual, audio, olfactory, or tactile—generated *by* the observer. A multiple-witness event would seem to dispel the idea that the event comes from the observer, but some psychologists claim that mass hysteria can produce visions and ghostly manifestations. A very large number of the stories I have collected about Gettysburg are accounts from two or more individuals witnessing the same event. Often, the first individual will not mention the event to the second unless the second initiates the discussion. The first individual will then have the other tell the details of the event in order to compare them with their own recollection of the experience. Usually, the similarity of their independent observations is remarkable beyond coincidence.

Still other researchers theorize that highly emotional human experiences leave a psychic impression upon the surrounding area: the walls of a house, or the ground, or rocks and surrounding, surviving trees near where the traumatic event happened. This is what I would classify as a residual haunting, something left over from the extreme expenditure of emotion.

But physically, scientifically, how can this happen?

Joe Farrell, while accompanying the late Cecil Downing on an investigation of ley lines in the Triangular Field, suggested that all the granite and its composite quartz predominant on the Gettysburg battlefield may have something to do with capturing the energy of the slain soldiers. He correctly explained that humans are driven by electricity: brain functions, muscular activity, the nervous system, even the skin, are all driven by, or are conductors of, the natural electrical impulses generated within our bodies. It was discovered that when the human brain is functioning at its peak, it generates enough electrical energy to power a light bulb. When *in extremis*—the point of death—there cannot be a time of more intense electrical energy coursing through the body. But how could this electrical energy affect rock?

The answer is on your wrist. Most of us wear quartz watches. A tiny battery, smaller than your pinky fingernail, causes a quartz crystal in the watch to vibrate steadily at 30,000 times per second, thereby allowing you to tell time from it.

Many of us, in an elementary school science project, created "crystal radios," based upon the receptivity of a rock—crystal—to subtle electromagnetic radio waves transmitted through the atmosphere. Capacitors—used to store electricity in electronic devices—are made of various materials such as epoxy, ceramics, polystyrene, polypropylene, mica (a rock), plastic, and even air. Many natural healers recognize the ability of rock—particularly quartz—to affect the health and well-being of individuals through focusing the electromagnetic energy of the universe.

So, electricity does affect rock—the quartz within the granite at Gettysburg—and may be the answer to the hauntings . . .at least at Gettysburg.[4]

There appears to be some scientific evidence for the notion that dying organisms emit extraordinary amounts of energy. Physicist Janusz Slawinki discovered that as cells perish and their genetic material starts to unravel, a powerful jolt of electromagnetic energy in the form of ionization, more than a thousand times greater than their normal resting state, is released. He called it a "light shout," and the energy released is apparently measurable with the proper instruments.[5]

According to the accepted laws of thermodynamics, energy in the universe is neither lost nor gained but merely changes form. A paper written by Dr. A. A. Mills of Leicester University demonstrates how extreme conditions such as torture, force oxygen atoms apart releasing tiny pinpricks of atomic energy.[6] Certainly a man wounded and dying must be considered as undergoing a certain kind of physical "torture."

One must also remember that many of the old houses in Gettysburg—because it is Gettysburg—have been consciously preserved, where in other towns old houses are torn down. Some 200 out of the 400 original structures remain. With 51,000 casualties, many, if not most of the buildings were used as hospitals, operating rooms, recovery rooms, and perhaps even as burial sites in the earthen-floored cellars. As well, consider the construction materials of the houses in Gettysburg. A large number have walls made out of the granite and quartz-bearing fieldstones, or at least are built upon foundations made of those fieldstones. Many of the existing houses are made of local, salmon-colored brick, which also contains minerals and elements amenable to the absorption of energy. Much of the wood framing of the houses, and often the bloodstained floorboards, remain as part of the structures. It is as if all of Gettysburg, from geology to dwelling places, is one big storage battery for the energy of the dead.

The Old Jail Now the Borough Building

The Old Schoolhouse

HOW TO INVESTIGATE THE PARANORMAL

Since the publication of *Ghosts of Gettysburg,* there has been a rash of amateur "Ghost Investigators" swarming the fields of the National Park at Gettysburg, rushing from one place to another before the park closes. Some have even tried to sneak onto the National Park after closing, believing that the only haunted area in Gettysburg is enclosed by the National Park Service boundaries. Invariably, they have gotten caught, ticketed, and managed to upset more than a few park rangers.

Flashes from cameras explode with the rapidity of musketry as individuals snap away, hoping to get photos of "orbs" or "vortexes" and ending up with close-up pictures of the dust they just stirred up and the amazing "flesh-colored" vortex they insist is *not* their finger in front of the lens.

They stay out in the rain and snow and are astounded at the multiple orbs that clutter their photos so thickly one cannot see the background. They hurriedly put out the cigarette they were just smoking to be amazed at the white, fog-like wisp of paranormal mist captured on their digital camera.

Obviously, they have *not* captured the spirits of the dead in their photographs, and actually have set back any legitimate investigations. Any true knowledge of the paranormal has been sacrificed just for the individual to say, inaccurately, "Look, here's a ghost at Gettysburg."

In spite of the tens of thousands of anecdotal pieces of data on the existence of the supernatural collected over the centuries, and their careful interpretation, and the thousands of photos of unexplainable images taken under the strictest protocols, de-bunkers, such as they are, will try to throw all of that out the window with one provable mistake. Therefore, it is imperative to conduct an investigation under the strictest of scientific orderliness, starting out with historical research of the site and ending with the accurate recording of data for further study by other researchers who follow.

While investigating the paranormal involves some intangibles, such as intuition and spontaneity, so does "legitimate" science, as even Einstein admitted. Historians, with their strict adherence to documented "fact" admit that, in arriving at their ultimate conclusions, a good deal of intangible past knowledge becomes part of their interpretations.

So, how does one conduct an investigation into the paranormal?

RESEARCH

Legitimate paranormal investigators will thoroughly research an area suspected of being haunted: the history, the people who once lived there, the deaths of those involved with the site, any violence associated with the site, and past reports of paranormal events.

There are several reasons you want to examine the history of a suspected haunted site.

First, this information can lead to possible explanations of present day hauntings. Second, knowledge of the events and people associated with the site can be a tool to help contact or bring out any residual entities remaining at the site.

Third, while a house known for paranormal activity was built within the last few years, the earth upon which it was built may have connections with a sordid and violent past. For example, modern houses in a section of Gettysburg known as "Colt Park" have been known to, upon occasion, emit a rancid odor from closets; minutes later it is gone. The houses themselves have no history of death or violence, but the ground upon which they were built was once part of bloody Pickett's Charge and was the burial site of many of those killed in that massive holocaust. Hence, the probable source for the paranormal activity.

Finally, research will give you names of individuals who owned or were associated with a structure or site. When one is attempting to photograph, or especially record Electronic Voice Phenomena (E.V.P.), results seem to be better when individuals are addressed by name. For example, some of the best E.V.P. I have ever recorded was at the Jennie Wade Birth House (not the Jennie Wade House where she was shot) on Baltimore Street just north of Breckenridge Street. (Recalling your history of Gettysburg, you will remember that Jennie Wade was the only civilian killed in the three-day battle.) The session went like this:

Mark: "John Pfoutz, are you here?"
Answer (male voice): "Yes."
Mark: "John Pfoutz, you owned this house, didn't you?"
Answer: "Yes, sir, I did!"
Mark: "Mary Ann Filby Wade, did you feel poor here?"
Answer (female voice): "Good Lord, yes."
Mark: "Did you and your daughters have to work hard?"
Answer: "Yes!"
Mark: "Did you work hard sewing?"
Answer: "Yes."[1]

I attribute the success of this particular session to the preliminary research I did on the house. I discovered that a man named John Pfoutz owned the house and that the Wades rented from him at the time of Jennie Wade's birth. Jennie's mother's maiden name was Mary Ann Filby, information also uncovered during the research process. Jennie's father had been incarcerated by the law, throwing Mrs. Wade and her daughters into virtual poverty. They took over Wade's tailoring business and worked hard sewing to make ends meet.

My research gave us something to talk about.

If indeed we are connecting to once-living humans' personalities, should they not be treated with respect and politeness? How would you like it if someone suddenly burst into your house, acting like they could not see you, smoking a cigarette, flashing a camera and started shouting, "Is anybody here?" Knowing names and addressing individuals is certainly better than "intruding."

Where does one research the names and events of Gettysburg that will prove useful in a paranormal investigation?

Fortunately, the Battle of Gettysburg is one of the most documented events in human history. Volumes have been written about the people living in Gettysburg at the time, of the officers and men who fought in the battle, and of the sites, well-known and obscure, where men struggled and died. Many of the more readable sources are listed at the end of this book in the "Resources" section. It would be wise to consult these books before doing an investigation at Gettysburg.

Later in this book, in the "Haunted Sites" sections, you will notice I have included some names of individual people who fought in the haunted areas, names of states from which the regiments came, and other specific information, like nicknames. In other words, I have done some of the initial historical research for you. Use these names and personal tidbits when you are attempting to photograph or gather E.V.P.

ATTITUDE

This brings us to one of the intangible aspects of "Ghost Hunting." We have already established the fact that you would personally object to suddenly hearing a voice rudely shouting at you, or calling your name and laughing, or making fun of you as if you were not even there. Would you bother to answer?

Probably not. If entities on "The Other Side" maintain any of their human characteristics and personalities (as most researchers believe) they would still be sensitive to someone barging in on their peace and quiet. This would especially be true of the former denizens of a much more sophisticated, conservative society, such as Victorian America—the Civil War period.

And, most importantly, an attitude of respect certainly is due the Civil War soldiers who put their lives on the line—and lost them—at Gettysburg. Therefore, whenever you enter the "Hallowed Ground" over which they fought and for which they died, whether you are investigating the paranormal or studying the history of the area and the great deeds done here, please conduct yourself with respectfulness.

As my writings about the encampments of reenactors during the anniversary commemorations of the battle and during the filming of the movie "Gettysburg" attest, just as we can see what appear to be spirits of the dead upon occasion, it seems that, as well, they can see us. That is perhaps why so many reenactor encampments teem with stories of "the most authentic-looking reenactor" passing through the camp. . .then vanishing, or campfires being seen where there was no encampment, only to disappear as inspectors approach. It seems as if the spirits feel more comfortable in the midst of those who look familiar, as they and their friends looked so long ago, before there was a battle at this place called Gettysburg. . .before they were sent on their one-way journey to eternity.

I have gone into the Triangular Field armed with a Civil War Drill Manual and a roster of the names of the men who fought there. I have called the men to attention, read off their names, and have gotten E.V.P. which sounded like voices answering me, voices that could not be heard while they were being recorded.

Other investigators have tried playing Civil War Era music to "relax" the spirits, make them feel more like they are once again alive in their own time.

I took a tuning fork, registered to the vibration of "om," the universal tone of the earth and all creation according to Eastern religion, and set it vibrating in the Triangular Field. Whether it was the tuning fork, or my calling the men of the 15th Georgia to attention to receive their pay using the Confederate Manual, or reading from their regimental roster the dead and wounded left in the once horrid field, that produced results that night, I will never know. But they responded, unheard by my ear, recorded for posterity on my digital recorder as a muffled "Yes, sir," and sharp, irritated roars, sounding like angry frustration.

EQUIPMENT

It is very likely that you came to Gettysburg to visit the battlefield, learn a little history, and relax at one of the fine motels or restaurants in the area. You may even have come to Gettysburg not realizing that there was a second side to the town and battlefield, a side steeped in the paranormal: the spirit side of Gettysburg. A paranormal investigation or "ghost hunt" was not even on your agenda, until you got here and realized that there are things to learn in Gettysburg in addition to its storied battle history.

Even if you have come to Gettysburg unprepared to hunt ghosts, you probably brought with you the right equipment to do a basic investigation.

As many paranormal investigators will state, the most important piece of ghost hunting equipment is the investigator himself. The investigator's preliminary research, attitude, adherence to protocol, attention to detail, experience, common sense, and raw intuition are the most potent pieces of equipment in his or her arsenal.

There are, however, some pieces of equipment that are more useful in first locating paranormal anomalies, and others in recording them for later analysis. Therefore, field equipment for a paranormal investigation can generally be divided into two categories: 1) Detecting equipment and 2) Recording equipment.

DETECTING EQUIPMENT

Detecting equipment will help you know if a particular site is active at that moment. This equipment can range from sophisticated Electromagnetic Field Meters to one's own psychic sensitivity.

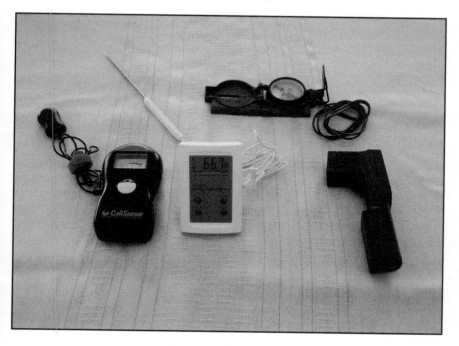

Detecting Equipment

Investigators have had great success at Gettysburg with infrared thermal scanners (also known as non-contact thermometers) or remote temperature sensors. A thermal scanner will detect temperature at a distance using infrared light. Since many accounts of ghostly encounters mention feeling a chill in the air, a thermal scanner can be a good way of locating spirit energies. Investigators will do a 360 degree sweep with a thermal scanner to see if there are any severe anomalies in the temperature. Where there are large variations in temperature, they will take a picture. Often the picture will reveal an orb or paranormal mist.

Many paranormal investigators use a digital thermometer with a probe to detect changes in temperature indicating the possible presence of an entity.

Rick Fisher, while doing a sweep of the field of Pickett's Charge, got numerous readings on his thermal scanner as low as minus three degrees, when the ambient temperature around him was between 30 and 33 degrees. As I previously related, when I walked over to investigate where he detected the temperature anomalies, I felt the cold. While I stood there, others took pictures which showed orbs "gathering" curiously around me.

Using a thermal scanner also confirms that there is a type of "heat" energy associated with orbs. Photographs indicate they have some sort of light energy, either generated by themselves or stimulated by the infrared or flash lighting used by cameras. They also may have reflective properties indicating they contain some "real" substance.

Electromagnetism is another attribute of orbs and paranormal mists— what investigators are convinced are the physical manifestations of spirits in our world. Therefore, some investigators like to carry electromagnetic field (EMF) meters. I have captured many orbs on film after a fellow investigator has seen a spike on the EMF meter. Some speculate that this is why the tiny hairs on the back of one's neck or arms stand in the presence of spirit energy. Others point to this electromagnetism, in the form of static electricity, as the reason why dogs and cats are sensitive to ghost phenomena. Their fur reacts to the infinitesimal electromagnetic charge associated with ghosts and the animals act strangely.

EMF meters are readily available through scientific equipment catalogues or on the internet. Some have several sensitivity settings; some are multi-field; some have audible alarms whenever an electromagnetic field is detected.

If the cost of an EMF meter is prohibitive, a compass may be used to detect magnetism in an area. When the compass spins, you may be in the realm of influence of a spirit. I once saw a small bar magnet mounted on a gimbal so it would rotate toward whatever axis to which it was attracted. The only problem with compasses or magnets is that they have no audible warning and so must be watched to detect any anomalies.

CAUTION! A sensitive EMF meter can be set off by exactly what they're supposed to read: electromagnetic fields given off by computers, televisions, microwave ovens, reading lamps and household electrical wires. Make sure you are aware of other fields near where you are using the meter to prevent false readings. Even compasses can be thrown off by ambient electromagnetic waves.

RECORDING EQUIPMENT

The study of the paranormal is by nature controversial. Sighting ghosts, hearing phantom footsteps, smelling the perfume of a long dead woman from a by-gone era, usually meant one was immediately classified as delusional. While history is filled with accounts of ghostly encounters, they have almost always officially been relegated to fiction and the imagination.

But therein lies the problem. History *is* filled with accounts of paranormal phenomena. Virtually every generation from every nation and tribe and society throughout history has its stories of the dead re-visiting the living. They may all have different reasons for the visitation, but they are still accounts of the dead coming back. Are *that* many people throughout history delusional? It is highly doubtful.

Recording Equipment

In the past, we had to take the word of the individual as the only proof of a paranormal event they had experienced. Today, with some basic equipment, we can capture evidence of the paranormal for later analysis or validation. You probably already have this equipment: A camera and an audio recorder.

What ghost hunters call "orbs" or "ectoplasm," "paranormal mist" or "vortexes," are, in their opinion, evidence of spirit activity. Usually they cannot be seen by the human eye. Some theorize that spirit energy is in a wavelength impossible to see with the human eye (although some psychics and other highly sensitive people claim they can see orbs or paranormal mist with the naked eye.) The shutter of a camera works so quickly that, if spirit activity is present, it can be captured.

CAMERAS

Many researchers like to use a digital camera because it gives them immediate results. Digital cameras are also nice because you can record almost an infinite number of shots by deleting those showing no evidence of paranormal activity. Images from digital cameras can be easily downloaded to computers and shared with others, enlarged, or "enhanced," and studied more closely.

Standard cameras, from expensive 35mm types to disposable cameras, have all yielded results when the conditions were right. The only drawback is that you have to wait—sometimes several days, sometimes only an hour—to see the print. The result is that, since you are "photographing blind," you do not know if an area is active while you are physically there.

In other words, for your first time "Ghost Hunting," the camera you brought with you to Gettysburg is fine.

Random camera shots—"from the hip" so to speak—often produce good results. Rick Fisher, renowned ghost hunter and Director of the Pennsylvania Paranormal Society, uses a "sixth sense" to tell him when to snap a photo. He will get a feeling, intuitively turn a certain way, snap a picture, and come up with a photo containing orbs or paranormal mist. Sometimes just turning around and snapping a picture will render a successful "orb" photo, since they seem to follow people as if curious.

Investigating in Gettysburg, particularly inside a building, we have found that after investigators have set up their equipment, then leave the room, there is a flurry of paranormal activity. It is as if the researchers frighten the entities (which are apparently shy) into retreating, then once the researchers are gone, the entities return to see what was going on.

The point is, do not be afraid to use your own creativity and sensitivity when photographing in a suspected active area.

VIDEO CAMERAS

A video camera is always a good thing to have on an investigation. Some of the country's most respected paranormal investigators will videotape their entire session. If any paranormal events do occur, the video can be reviewed in order to demonstrate that no hoax was involved. I always videotape my investigations, sometimes using two video cameras—one hand-held and the other one on a tripod—to intercept accusations that things were staged. In addition, you just never know when the video camera, which is running all the time, will pick up something when your still camera is at rest.

Sony, as well as some other companies, makes a camcorder with NightShot®. Canon has its "Super Night Shooting Mode," and Panasonic its MagicVu™. They all give you the opportunity to make videos in complete darkness with infrared lighting. Some even come with an infrared add-on light to extend the range. I have seen them capture orbs—and, in an extremely rare case, E.V.P. *and* orbs—in motion.

AUDIO EQUIPMENT

At least 60 percent of all ghost encounters are auditory in nature. Along with footsteps, music, and battle noises, some witnesses at Gettysburg claim to have heard voices: orders being shouted, moans of the wounded, names whispered in their ears, and babies crying.

Electronic Voice Phenomenon (E.V.P.) is the recording of a voice for which there is no apparent source. Many believe the voice belongs to the dead.

Attempts at communicating with the dead are not new. Grief-stricken mourners will attempt to talk to the immediately deceased, not believing they could have died; people will speak at gravesites to long dead relatives as a self-comforting measure; over the centuries, individuals have recruited psychics—some legitimate, some bogus—to help them talk to dead loved ones. An entire "industry"—Spiritualism—grew in the 19th Century out of relatives' desire to communicate with the generation killed during the Civil War. Renowned inventors Thomas Edison and Guglielmo Marconi worked on machines to attempt to communicate with the dead.

Some of the first E.V.P. was recorded in 1959 on regular magnetic tape by Friedrich Jurgenson who, while recording bird songs alone in an open field, inadvertently recorded a male voice expertly discussing in Norwegian, nocturnal bird songs. Repeated experiments produced more voices recorded on the tape, although unheard by Jurgenson while he was recording. Eventually he ruled out extraneous sources such as radio or television broadcasts—the voices relayed personal information and even began giving Jurgenson instructions on how to more effectively record the bird songs! A Latvian researcher named Konstantin Raudive worked with Jurgenson and eventually recorded over 100,000 voices, finally publishing his results in 1971 in his book *Breakthrough.*

There are several techniques for recording E.V.P. One technique is to start a tape running and simply walk away. The site is important: battlefields, graveyards, or buildings, with a haunted past are more likely sources of E.V.P. Reviewing the entire tape will reveal if any extraneous voices were recorded. Shelley Sykes, co-author of the series *The Gettysburg Ghost Gang,* uses this technique with a compact reel-to-reel tape recorder with remarkable success.

It is important to always use a brand new tape so that previously recorded information will not "bleed" through. You may also want to employ a witness to, or videotape, the unwrapping of the tape, so no one can cry "fraud." Some investigators insist that you use a remote microphone as well, since many reel-to-reel cassette tape recorders' motors make noise that may be mistaken for E.V.P.

Another technique is to ask questions into the recorder, then pause for answers. Some of the most remarkable—and somewhat disturbing— experiments that I have done were with a credit-card sized Panasonic Model No. RR-DR60. The digital recorder is set on voice activation mode. While I ask a question, the electronic numbers in the display roll forward and the recorder's LED light glows steadily to indicate something is being recorded. When I stop talking, the light flashes on and off (to indicate that it is in voice activation mode but not recording anything) and the numbers cease to roll. Then I pause for 30 to 50 seconds.[2] Suddenly, in total silence, the light begins to glow steadily and the numbers begin to roll. The seemingly impossible is taking place—something is being recorded that cannot be heard.

Upon playback, various qualities of noises can be heard. Sometimes there is just a loud (extremely loud!) roar, as if something were very angry or, more to the point, frustrated. It is guttural, explosive, and can be painful to the ears if the recorder is held too close. Other sounds are background noises, like the "white noise" heard during a party: a sort of murmur, a mixing of voices, indistinguishable as individual voices or phrases, but a low mumbling behind everything. While these sounds are not understandable as words or sentences, they are still remarkable. *They are noises recorded in complete silence!* There should be nothing on the recorder since there was nothing to be heard during the recording.

I set a new Panasonic digital recorder on "voice-activated" and placed it on a twelve-foot thick brick casement sill at Fort Delaware. No one was around, and yet, for 18 seconds the recorder captured strange, muffled sounds out of time.

WARNING! Absolutely no smoking during an investigation! Respect others already doing an investigation. When someone in your team is doing E.V.P., be quiet. If you are trying to get E.V.P. and someone talks or coughs, identify it on the recorder so it won't be confused with legitimate E.V.P.

*　　　*　　　*

Do not be discouraged if you are not one of those sensitive enough to pick up on the paranormal world. Many people have visited Gettysburg scores of times—many have lived here all their lives—and never had a paranormal experience.

Although I have lived in Gettysburg for over thirty years, I still can count only four or five personal paranormal experiences. Some people come to Gettysburg and have an experience right away, though they have never had one before in their life. Others, often while on one of our *Ghosts of Gettysburg Candlelight Walking Tours®,* have heard, seen or smelled what is obviously an out-of-time event. Yet someone standing right next to them will have experienced nothing.

The answer as to why some of us experience the paranormal and others do not, is that we are all born with natural differences in perception. Psychic abilities, or even just sensitivity to psychic happenings, are dissimilar in all of us. Some of us have better hearing, some better eyesight, or a better singing voice. Some are born with a more acute sensitivity to the paranormal. The customers on our tours are a good example: When one person smells pipe tobacco burning and someone right next to them does not, it is merely an indication that one is more sensitive to the paranormal than another.

The encouraging part is that many experts agree that one can develop one's psychic sensitivities.

But the fact that someone who has never had a paranormal experience in their life, until they get to Gettysburg, is an indication of only one thing: it is the *place*, Gettysburg, that contains the spirits they can experience.

WHERE TO LOOK FOR GHOSTS IN GETTYSBURG

Numerous sites on the National Park can be considered haunted. Time and time again people have reported hearing drums, fifes, orders being shouted, cries for help, rolling volleys of musketry, cannons discharging, the unique sound of hundreds of men on the march, and large numbers of horses galloping by, when none could be seen. Others have reported seeing individual soldiers wandering around or walking next to them, as if they were reenactors, then vanishing into thin air–something reenactors have not yet been able to accomplish. Others still have seen entire battalions of men, march, maneuver, wheel off into the woods, and disappear. Lines of fire—like musketry—flash in the woods at night, with no sound accompanying the flashes.

While "The Battlefield"—synonymous to many people with the "National Park"—is obviously a place where a great deal of violence has taken place, do not overlook the fact that the town of Gettysburg, and many of the small towns surrounding it, were all victims of the largest campaign and battle to ever occur on the North American continent in recorded history.[1]

WARNING! Make sure to verify the visitation hours for the National Park. There are no exceptions! Do not plan to be in the park outside of the posted hours. Many of the historic structures on the National Park are inhabited by park rangers or private individuals. They are not open to the public. Respect the privacy of those living on the park.

Mass Burial Sites

The men who were killed at Gettysburg were first buried near where they fell. Bodies were gathered into central burial locations. In many cases, long trenches were dug, bodies rolled in, and covered with a thin layer of dirt. On Culp's Hill, 108 Confederates were buried in one trench.[2] Lt. Thomas Galwey from Ohio, on July 5, 1863, along the Emmitsburg Road after Pickett's Charge, saw men buried in trenches long enough to hold fifty to one hundred dead.[3] Often, shallow single graves were dug, the body placed in the pit and covered with just enough soil to dissuade scavengers. No attempts at embalming were made, and coffins were usually the blanket the men carried with them on the march when they were alive.

Identification was sketchy, since there were no government issued "dog-tags" as in future wars. Confederates often went unidentified, because their army marched off in retreat and left many of their dead to the care of the Union soldiers who retained the battlefield. Even Federal soldiers, if their unit moved from the position where they had died in the fighting, were left to the care of strangers who had no idea who these men were, other than what state they came from—and only if they wore state-crested buttons or breastplates.

Maps of the burial sites were made, often by caring comrades who knew the family of the deceased might want the body back. The first official map of the burial sites, made by S. G. Elliott, shows long rows of hundreds of graves. Others made maps, but a listing of 1,100 Union soldiers' burial sites by John G. Frey, although incomplete, was helpful. Dr. J. W. C. O'Neal's catalogue of about 1,100 Confederate burials also added to the knowledge of burials. The most thorough study was made by Samuel Weaver, one of the first individuals contracted to remove the Union dead from the farmers' fields. He kept records of where and how many bodies were buried in different spots.

Dr. Rufus Weaver, Samuel Weaver's son, "inherited," at first reluctantly, his father's duties after Samuel's death in 1871. By then organizations from the southern states having soldiers buried at Gettysburg were trying to bring the remains home. During the early 1870's Rufus Weaver removed some 3,320 remains and shipped them back to the southern states from which they began their short journey through life that ended at Gettysburg.[4]

The question I, and other park rangers, were frequently asked by visitors who were interested in what happened to the dead at Gettysburg was, "Did they get all the bodies?"

The "official" Park Service line in the early 1970's was, "Yes, all the bodies were recovered and either re-interred in the National Cemetery or sent to cemeteries in the South." This, we now know, was not correct.

Estimates of between a few hundred and over a thousand "missing" bodies are as close as anyone can get to the actual number of soldiers still buried on the battlefield. Bodies—or rather bones and fragments of clothing—are still being found into this new century, and, no doubt, will continue to be in the years ahead.[5]

WARNING! The Soldier's National Cemetery and Evergreen Cemetery are <u>NOT</u> appropriate places for a paranormal investigation. Supremely brave men sacrificed their lives and futures, and in some cases, their very identities, so that we may enjoy the fruits of living in the United States. Good taste and decorum suggest that you pursue the hobby of paranormal investigating at the numerous other sites available.

PLACES OF GREAT SLAUGHTER

The field of "Pickett's Charge" on either side of the Emmitsburg Road was not only a massive gravesite, according to the Elliott maps and most other accounts, but was the scene of incredible butchery. It seems as if all the destructive elements of 19th Century warfare were focused upon that space, all within the short time it takes to walk nine-tenths of a mile and fight for your life for about ten minutes.

From the moment they stepped out of the woods on Seminary Ridge on the afternoon of July 3, 1863, the approximately 12,500 men in Longstreet's Assault came under artillery fire. Union gunners on Little Round Top thought it was like target practice. Men were ripped apart or pounded down against the ground as shells burst overhead; they were knocked over or gutted or had pieces of their bodies torn off as iron artillery "shot" bounded off the rocky ground and into the packed ranks. By the time they reached the Emmitsburg Road, they were struggling to keep their ranks in order.

They struck a stout post and five-rail fence at the road which would not budge as they tried to break it down with shoulders and musket butts. As they began to climb over, Union infantry rose from the stone wall at the crest of the ridge in front of them and fired as one man. The distance was the ideal killing range for the military rifled-musket of the era, and hundreds of one-ounce, soft lead, .58 caliber minie balls, traveling just under 900 feet per second, slammed into the mens' bodies and limbs and faces and heads. They tumbled senseless or in horrible agony into the road or back over the fence. Those who survived the artillery and initial infantry volleys continued across the road and up the gentle slope toward the stone wall, their flimsy cloth caps pulled low and heads bowed as if walking into a heavy rainstorm.

Most of the command structure had been shot away by now, so the men pushed their way, like a mob following their flags, up to the wall, driving some of the defenders back. In other areas they advanced to within a few yards of the cannons which, by now, had switched to canister—tin cans full of iron balls like huge shotgun shells—that ripped ranked men into mere pieces of flesh.

Some Confederates leapt the stone wall and were counter-attacked by organized Union regiments. The fighting was hand-to-hand, with men smashing each other over the head with muskets, rocks, fists, wrestling on the ground, firing point-blank into each other, falling, bleeding, dying among the struggling mass.

Slowly, like a vast wave receding, the surviving Confederates made their way back, leaving the space between the Union lines at the low stone wall and the Emmitsburg Road a mass of crimson gore.

The names of other places on the National Park where men were mowed down like ripe wheat are well known: McPherson's Ridge, Oak Ridge, Barlow's Knoll, Little Round Top, Devil's Den, Culp's Hill, East Cemetery Hill, The Peach Orchard, The Triangular Field, The Wheatfield, The Rose Farm.

As well, the places in the town of Gettysburg where men were shot down or suffered greatly are numerous: The Lutheran Seminary, Pennsylvania (now Gettysburg) College, Kuhn's Brickyard, Carlisle Street, Stratton Street, Washington Street, and Baltimore Street during the Union retreat on July 1; the sites of Colt Park, the Recreation Park, the Gettysburg Athletic Stadium where sports teams now compete, and the hundreds of buildings, both public and private, where the wounded lay for days in the July heat.

In essence, with some 175,000 men and boys attempting to kill one another for three days in July, 1863, nearly everywhere in and around the town of Gettysburg was battlefield.

HOSPITAL SITES

WARNING! Many of these sites and structures are privately owned. Please respect the owners' rights to privacy and avoid doing any investigations without permission of the owners.

Once the fighting began, aid stations were established. The sites were just behind the battle lines, usually in some woods near a stream for shade and water. After the walking wounded were treated, they made their way to field hospital sites, most often a nearby farmhouse with a barn, or some of the larger structures in and around the town of Gettysburg. The severely wounded went through the same procedure: first aid station, then to a field hospital, except that they were carried on stretchers by orderlies.

Often you will hear the generic name "Hospital Woods." There are a number of areas once used by surgeons as aid stations and are so named. The National Park Service purchased some of these sites for preservation, and most remain wooded to this day.

One road near Gettysburg (running between the Baltimore Pike and the Taneytown Road) is named "Hospital Road" for the large number of Union field hospitals that once occupied the barns and houses along it. At least one of the more modern homes seems to change hands just about every other year, and one must ask if this is evidence, perhaps, of some unsettled spirits reclaiming their right to occupancy of the land beneath it.[6]

Within the last fifteen years, the National Park Service has made an effort, largely using research from Gregory Coco's works on the aftermath of the battle, to mark the hospital sites with metal blue or gray signs, not only within the Park's boundaries, but outside the Park as well.

Hospital Site: McPherson Barn

After the battle, the surgeons realized that supplying the numerous field hospitals created a logistical nightmare, and so decided to bring all the wounded to a central location to recuperate and be sent home, or, sadly, die there. This large outdoor hospital was named Camp Letterman and was located about a mile east of Gettysburg on the York Road (now Route 30 East). In addition to being close to the railroad tracks (so that the wounded could be transported out of Gettysburg to larger cities to the east), it also contained shady woods, nice breezes, and a freshwater spring. A large cookhouse was erected, as well as quarters for surgeons, nurses, and members of the United States Sanitary Commission. There was also a deadhouse and embalmer's tent. Soon the land would sprout headboards in a cemetery adjacent to the 400 tents sheltering the wounded.

HAUNTED SITES ON THE EAST SIDE OF THE BATTLEFIELD

SPANGLER'S SPRING

Spangler's Spring has consistently proven to be a hotbed of paranormal activity. The area is historically known for changing hands several times during the battles on July 2 and July 3, 1863. From the records we know that Confederates from Steuart's Brigade (1st Maryland Battalion, 1st and 3rd North Carolina, and the 10th, 23rd, and 37th Virginia Infantry units) visited the Spangler's Spring area on the night of July 2. On the Union side, the 2nd Massachusetts, 46th Pennsylvania, 20th Connecticut, and 123rd New York all roamed the area that night as well.

The most famous ghost that inhabits Spangler's Spring is the "Woman in White." She has been seen by people so numerous that she has become a legend. At least three separate sightings have been documented in the *Ghosts of Gettysburg* series. She is seen as an upright column of mist that floats through the meadows around the Spring, stopping, apparently leaning over, then moving on. Because of this strange behavior, and because of renowned psychic Karyol Kirkpatrick's investigation, she has been tentatively identified as a nun whose order dressed in white, who came after the battle to care for the wounded. At Spangler's Spring, trapped by some quirk of supernature, she still seeks the dying nearly a century-and-a-half later.

Still others claim that she is the spirit of a spurned mistress, whose married lover led her on and finally rejected her, driving her to suicide at their meeting place, Spangler's Spring. She continues, to this day, to wander the meadows around the Spring, forever searching for the lover she lost in life.

There have been numerous sightings of "Shadow People" or "Dark Ghosts" in the woods on the hillside opposite Spangler's Spring.[1] This is a different type of entity from what we normally associate with ghosts, which are commonly seen as white or amorphous clouds of mist-like substance. "Shadow People" are dark beings that can be seen by the background light that they block as they float across the landscape. While some people have suggested it, there has been no reason to believe they represent evil.

Also in the vicinity of the Spring, a woman and a fellow investigator saw small, wispy, flying entities sweep towards them, then "chase" each other around and around a tree trunk.

Spangler's Spring

How to Get There

From Gettysburg's Lincoln Square, travel south on Baltimore Street, past the *Ghosts of Gettysburg Candlelight Walking Tours®* Headquarters on the corner of Breckenridge Street, and turn left on LeFever Street. Ahead of you will be the local Junior High School. Bear left and follow the road between the schools to the next stop sign. Turn right and follow the road around Culp's Hill to Spangler's Spring. Park in the area provided.

Tips on Investigating

Many psychic investigators have claimed that water is a conduit for the spirits of the dead. Although Spangler's Spring has been fed by Gettysburg Borough waterlines for years, the area still contains underground water in the form of water tables and springs. An appeal to the "Woman in White"—the eternally-caring nun who still feels the call to aid long-dead soldiers—may work to call her out. Use the names of the state regiments who fought around the Spring, as well, in your investigation. Be aware that "Dark Ghosts," and the unusual small bits of paranormal mist, apparently frequent the area. Watch for the unexpected!

CULP'S HILL AND THE TOWER

Culp's Hill became part of the battle action late on July 2, 1863, with an evening Confederate assault upon the Union right flank. The soldiers on both sides began a fight neither wished: as the sun set, darkness fell in the claustrophobic woods, and men fired at musket flashes, never knowing whether they were killing friend or foe.

According to Gregory Coco in his excellent book, *A Strange and Blighted Land, Gettysburg: The Aftermath of a Battle*, J. Howard Wert, an early visitor to the battlefield, described the "angle" in the Union line on Culp's Hill as covered more thickly with the dead of both armies than any other place he had seen on the battlefield. A good four acres around the "angle" was carpeted with the dead, so that one could hardly walk without stepping upon a body. On the Confederate side of the "angle" the slain were stacked almost to the height of the breastworks. He counted bodies three deep.[2]

The Angle at Culp's Hill

The road to the summit has produced strange flashes of light, seen both by the naked human eye and caught on film. Strange audible cries for help have echoed through the woods; investigation, even by park rangers, revealed no source. The steel tower at the summit has reverberated with phantom footsteps, and unexpected visitors have been known to appear on the tower platform and just as mysteriously disappear.[3]

How to Get There

From Gettysburg's Lincoln Square, travel south on Baltimore Street, past the *Ghosts of Gettysburg Candlelight Walking Tours*® Headquarters on the corner of Breckenridge Street, and turn left on LeFever Street. Ahead of you will be the local Junior High School. Bear left and follow the road between the schools to the next stop sign. Turn right and follow the road around Culp's Hill to Spangler's Spring. From Spangler's Spring follow the National Park Service signs toward the summit of Culp's Hill. Watch for the "angle" in the mounds representing the breastworks to the right of the road just past the Maryland Monument and the sign identifying Slocum Avenue. Park in designated areas only. To reach the tower which is at the summit of Culp's Hill, continue to follow the main road, bearing to the right at the junction of Slocum and Williams Avenues.

Tips on Investigating

Dusk is a good time to visit this section of the battlefield, since most of the commercial tours have been completed by then. Be certain to stop near the 1st Maryland Battalion Monument. Perhaps you'll have the courage to enter the woods just over the "angle" in the breastworks. Men of Brigadier General George H. Steuart's Brigade from Virginia, North Carolina, and, of course, Maryland, fought and died in the angle visible in the remnants of the breastworks. They battled New Yorkers in Brigadier General George S. Greene's Brigade. As you face the angle, to your right rear, the 5th Ohio fought, losing Lieutenant Henry C. Brinkman. Farther to the right of the 5th Ohio, the men of the 147th Pennsylvania observed a horrifying event in the fields before them. As the fighting died down, a severely wounded Confederate from the Maryland Battalion was seen laboriously loading his weapon. He was shot in the gut and obviously in excruciating pain. The Union soldiers aimed their weapons at him, but did not fire. Such suffering he endured pushed him past the edge of reason—even beyond religious prohibitions. As he finished loading, the Southerner put the muzzle of the weapon beneath his chin, touched the trigger with the ramrod, and ended his own life in the area near where the Maryland Monument stands today.

Confederate Brigadier General Steuart, who commanded some of the troops who fought here, seeing his young men shot down before him, wept in emotional agony as he babbled, "My poor boys! My poor boys!"[4]

Continue to the summit of Culp's Hill, climb the tower, pause, and listen for the phantom footsteps heard by a visitor one evening after a thunderstorm. He also felt the vibrations through the steel tower's structure, as leather-soled shoes made their way urgently up the stairs. Wait, as he did, for a human form to emerge from the stairwell, and, perhaps, be disappointed and confused as he was, when no one appears.

Or perhaps you will be lucky enough to see the beautiful, blonde, young woman who, without your knowing it, suddenly appears at the top of the tower, walks past you to the stairs, then disappears, never bothering to descend. You will notice her right away, if not for her beauty, then for the way she is dressed—like someone out of the 1950's. Her reason for being here? No one knows for sure, but perhaps an enterprising researcher will comb the Gettysburg police records of the 1950's and discover the tragic death by automobile accident, just a few hundred yards away from the tower, of one of the prettiest girls to graduate from the local high school. Could she be telling us that the Ghosts of Gettysburg are not confined to those killed in battle, but can visit from our more recent past?

EAST CEMETERY HILL

Late in the evening of July 2, 1863, Confederate Brigadier General Harry Hays launched an attack upon the Union lines on the east side of Cemetery Hill. Almost immediately, the men from the 5th, 6th, 7th, 8th, and 9th Louisiana regiments began taking artillery fire from Union gunners atop the hill. Within a few minutes, they were engaged with Union troops from the 107th and 75th Ohio and the 17th Connecticut posted along what is now called Wainwright Avenue. The fighting eventually became every soldier's nightmare—hand-to-hand. The men from Ohio and Connecticut were beaten back up the hill by Confederates who resorted to using their muskets as clubs when the action was too frantic to load. As Hays' men advanced up the slope of East Cemetery Hill, it was so dark that some of the soldiers could not tell whether the men they shot were friend or foe.

Hoke's Confederate Brigade, under the command of Colonel Isaac Avery and consisting of the 6th, 21st, and 57th North Carolina regiments attacked the Union line farther south along Wainwright Avenue, an area held by the 153rd Pennsylvania, and the 68th and 54th New York regiments. Colonel Avery was shot in the neck and went down in the darkness. Avery knew what it was like to be shot, having been wounded at Manassas and Malvern Hill. Perhaps he knew, as well, that this time it was different. This time the wound would kill him. In his last agonizing moments on this earth he wrote to his father: ". . .I died with my face to the enemy."[5]

As the North Carolinians passed along the open fields, Union artillery on their right flank fired double canister down the length of their line, ripping men to pieces. Still they came on.

Wielding his musket, a Yankee tried to club Colonel Godwin of the 57th North Carolina. Godwin parried the blow and slashed with his sword, slicing the man's head in half. (This occurred somewhere in the vicinity of the 33rd Massachusetts Regimental marker.)

East Cemetery Hill at Wainwright Avenue

Near Menchey's Spring, Sergeant Heinrich Michel, color-bearer of the 54th New York, was shot down dead. A little farther up the hill, Major Alexander Miller was shot carrying the colors of the 21st North Carolina; Private Jerry Bennett and Captain James F. Beall also carried the colors for a while, brave men one and all, considering the attrition rate among color-bearers.

How to Get There

From the Square, go south on Baltimore Street. Pass the *Ghosts of Gettysburg Candlelight Walking Tours*® Headquarters on your right and turn left on LeFever Street. With the Elementary School parking lot ahead of you, turn right and park in the lot on the left. The road you turned right on is the old Brickyard Lane, or Wainwright Avenue. Walk out that road—the Gettysburg Athletic Stadium will be on your left. Soon, on your right, you will see the hillside of East Cemetery Hill. Continuing on Wainwright Avenue, you will come to Menchey's Spring on the left, and a little farther on, the monument to the 33rd Massachusetts, the extreme left flank of the Confederate assault on East Cemetery Hill.

Menchey's Spring

Tips on Investigating

Once again use state names of regiments or nicknames. Ohioans were called "Buckeyes," and troops from North Carolina were called "Tarheels." Names of individuals may work as well. Dusk, when the attack took place, is a good time to explore this area.

WARNING! Remember, Wainwright Avenue is part of the National Park. Verify Park visitation hours.

HAUNTED SITES NORTH OF GETTYSBURG

IVERSON'S PITS

When Confederate Brigadier General Alfred Iverson launched an attack upon the Union line near the Mummasburg Road on the afternoon of July 1, 1863, he had not reconnoitered the ground over which his men were to advance. Neither did he send out skirmishers to discover any enemy ambushes. As it turned out, it was a fatal error for almost half of his 1400-man brigade. They marched across the Mummasburg Road and into the jaws of Hell.

Behind a wall on their left flank crouched hundreds of Union soldiers. When Iverson's men were a mere eighty yards away, the Union troops rose and fired as one man. Confederates toppled in crumpled heaps, like they were hit by a single scythe. When they came to bury them, it was noticed that a straight line could be sighted along their feet as they lay. Grave diggers dug a long shallow trench and rolled the men in, without honors or ceremony.

A decade later, the men's bodies went through another rough handling when they were disinterred and sent to cemeteries in the South. Like a bad memory, the disturbed earth remained as depressions in farmer Forney's field. His workmen, as dusk set in, would refuse to work near the depressions they had named "Iverson's Pits." There were rumors, whispers, of the workers hearing moans and crying, desperate orders being shouted, and the chilling sound of soft lead bullets thudding into flesh and cracking human bones.

How to Get There

From Gettysburg's Lincoln Square, follow Carlisle Street north and turn left at the light at Lincoln Avenue. Go two blocks and turn right on College Avenue. Follow College Avenue—which becomes the Mummasburg Road— over the hill and turn right into the Peace Light parking area on the right. Continue through the Peace Light parking lot and drive across the Mummasburg Road. Park in the lot past the National Park Service's small half-tower. Behind you is the wall Union soldiers used as defensive breastworks. There are several gaps in the wall where you can walk out into the field where Iverson's men were slaughtered.

Tips on Investigating

Any remnant of Iverson's Pits has long been washed away by time and the elements. However, since we know from the testimony of the Union soldiers that they opened fire at about eighty yards and that they were stationed behind the low stone wall that currently runs to the west of the parking lot near the National Park Service's half-tower, it is easy to estimate about where "The Pits" were.

Iverson's Brigade was, to a man, North Carolinians: the 5th, 12th, 20th, and 23rd North Carolina Infantry Regiments. The 5th and 20th were on the left of their line and took the brunt of the Union infantry fire. The 20th lost Lieutenant Colonel Slough and Major J. S. Brooks, as well as Lieutenant Williams, wounded almost in the first volley. From the 23rd fell Colonel Christie, to die later of his wounds. Their Lieutenant Colonel Johnson was wounded, but perhaps worst of all was their Major Blacknall, who took a bullet through the mouth and neck in the very first volley.

WARNING! Iverson's Pits is on National Park Service property and is closed to traffic after the posted visitation hours.

OAK RIDGE

In the afternoon of the first day of the battle, brave men of the Union Army held Oak Ridge as long as humanly possible, until the overwhelming pressure from Confederate assaults forced them back across the fields now used for play by the young men and women of Gettysburg College. Some of the men from Maine ended up making a gallant stand in the railroad cut to the south of the Mummasburg Road, but the rest tumbled back into Gettysburg, and to the high ground to the south of town.

As if they are trying to remind us of what they left here, strange beings are still seen and bizarre things still occur on the ridge that runs southward from the Peace Light.

A Union officer has been seen—not once, but a number of times—galloping along the ridge, oblivious to those in odd-looking (to him) modern clothing being conveyed in strange, wheeled contraptions. He is on a mission, apparently, to deliver a message. Just as suddenly as he appears, he vanishes, absorbed back into the cleft in time from where he mysteriously emerged.

Then there were the two sisters who, on a cold winter's night, took a walk along Doubleday Avenue...and into another world. As they passed the woods in the dark of night, when the cold would have driven most into shelter, they heard talking and singing. Curious, they entered the woods. The closer they got to the sound, the farther away it moved. Just as they began to feel lost, they heard what can only be described as an agonizing scream. Then, as if horror had done its worst and left only its memory, there was tortured sobbing.

The sobbing continued. Then came a call to arms, to "Get up, get up. Go! Go!" More screams, more sobbing, and suddenly, through the darkened night, "Charge!"

They ran in panic from those woods, not understanding, but absolutely certain of what they had just heard.[1]

How to Get There

From the area near the half-tower, continue along Doubleday Avenue. On the right you will pass—and may want to stop at—the monument to the 11th Pennsylvania and their little canine mascot "Sallie." Farther down the ridge, where the road curves to the right, you will enter the woods.

Tips on Investigating

This would be a good area to attempt to get Electronic Voice Phenomena. Although there is no official record of any field hospital being set up there, the area was fought over by the 76th and 95th New York and 56th Pennsylvania, as well as men from Mississippi and North Carolina. The woods are original— at least these are the descendants of the trees that made up the woods fought through during the battle and which sheltered those units' wounded.

WARNING! The area contains a number of private homes. Please respect the privacy of the residents.

BARLOW'S KNOLL

The extreme right flank of the Union line on July 1, 1863, was anchored on a small hill just a few hundred yards north of the county poor house— known as the "Alms House"—near the road to Harrisburg. Just below the crest of the hill is the Alms House Cemetery. Late in the afternoon the Federal line collapsed, in part because the Confederates outnumbered the Federals at the little hill. Union Major General Francis Barlow was shot and went down on the hill. Although there were literally hundreds of others killed and wounded on the rise, from that day it has been know as "Barlow's Knoll."

Young Lieutenant Bayard Wilkeson commanded the Union artillery battery upon the knoll. He seemed to be everywhere on his white horse, adjusting his battery line, making sure his men had ammunition, checking with superiors, but most of all, encouraging his men and making sure they were getting the maximum effect with their pieces.

His efficiency was noticed by his superiors. Unfortunately, it was noticed by the enemy, too. In a rare instance, Confederate gunners were ordered to take out the active officer on the white horse. This they did. Wilkeson was blown off his horse, horribly wounded. His leg was virtually amputated by a shell and hung by only sinew. It slowed him as he crawled to the Alms House for medical help, so he took out his pocket knife and finished the job. He later died of his wounds.

Barlow's Knoll

Though the Alms House is long gone, the cemetery is still there resting cheerlessly, forlornly, on the hill. Older locals call it by the Biblical name "Potter's Field," after the field purchased with the thirty pieces of silver Judas received for betraying Christ. In Jerusalem, the land bought with the blood money was set aside for the burial of strangers and the poor. Appropriately— both for Jerusalem and Gettysburg—it was called the Field of Blood forever after.

Recent sightings on the knoll have taken an ominous turn. Observed among the low tombstones of "Potter's Field" have been "Shadow People" or "Dark Ghosts." They have been seen moving across the road which loops around the cemetery, sometimes entering the cemetery itself. Some speculate that they are the remnants of the poor souls who, in this life, were estranged from society because of poverty or mental instability and are fated to roam the fields north of Gettysburg forever, knowing nothing about the great battle that took place over their very graves. Of course, with all the death and destruction dealt by the military combatants on this little hill, restless spirits other than those of the poor may roam here as well, seeking loyal comrades-in-arms forever.

Potter's Field

How to Get There

From Lincoln Square in Gettysburg drive north on Carlisle Street. After going through the traffic light at Lincoln Avenue and passing Broadway, you will begin to head out of town. Playing fields for Gettysburg College will be on your left and "Green Acres" County Home will be on your right. Turn right at the first crossroads (Howard Avenue) and you will be heading toward Barlow's Knoll.

Tips on Investigating

A large number of the men who fought on Barlow's Knoll were German immigrants. Some of the men were from New York, Ohio, Pennsylvania, Connecticut, Wisconsin, and Illinois. If you know any German, this would be a good place to try it, since a large number of the men spoke the language.

You may want to use some of the names of the officers involved in the fighting on Barlow's Knoll. General Francis Barlow, who was grievously wounded there, would be one to call on. Bayard Wilkeson would be another, having been shot down in the prime of his life, suffering horribly and dying far too young. During Wilkeson's fight, four of his men were wounded and one, Private Charles F. Hoefer, died from the effects of an artillery shell landing much too close. From the 153rd Pennsylvania, as they were advancing toward Barlow's

Knoll, Lieutenant William M. Beaver was shot close to the heart. Mortally wounded, July 1, 1863, would be his last day on earth.

During the Union retreat from Barlow's Knoll, the 153rd Pennsylvania was flanked on the left and the right and endured a crossfire from Confederates from John B. Gordon's Brigade. But slaughter was not confined to just the northern forces. As one Confederate wrote after the battle, "Men were being mown down in great numbers on both sides." The 4th Georgia lost its Lieutenant Colonel Winn, killed in the Confederate sweep over Barlow's Knoll.

The Yankees stubbornly attempted to hold on to the high ground. The 17th Connecticut counter-attacked, led by their doomed commander, Lieutenant Colonel Douglas Fowler. He met a horrible fate where the flagpole stands today on Barlow's Knoll. An artillery shell struck him in the head, decapitating him and splattering his brains upon his adjutant. At nearly the same instant, Captain James E. Moore's life was extinguished.[2]

WARNING! The Barlow's Knoll area (to the east of the Carlisle Road) and Howard Avenue (to the west of the Carlisle Road) are two of the few government-owned roads that are still accessible after the park closes. Visitors, however, are discouraged from stopping and parking after hours. It is recommended that you finish your investigation before the posted closing time.

HAUNTED SITES ON THE WEST SIDE OF THE BATTLEFIELD

PICKETT'S CHARGE

For decades, the Point of Woods, just to the south of the Virginia Memorial, was alleged to be haunted. Photos in my personal collection show strange lights—golden orbs and a gold crucifix mysteriously floating in the woods—in the area of the Memorial and the Point of Woods. It was here where orbs, as documented by Pennsylvania Paranormal Society founder Rick Fisher's thermal scanner, began to gather around me accompanied by an incredible drop in temperature, so much so that my fingers began to ache within a few seconds.[1]

Point of Woods

Others have spoken of descending into the swales that cross the field where Pickett's men marched to their doom and, even though it is a hot day, feel a chilling cold, so cold their breath actually condenses in the chill.[2]

Phantom units have been seen—and then been seen to disappear—as they marched across the field. An individual soldier's presence is confirmed by eyewitnesses; then, in the next second, so is his transportation into another dimension as the witnesses watch, astounded.

The Codori House on the Emmitsburg Road, where General Pickett supposedly stood with his staff to watch his ill-fated assault, has echoed in modern times with the footsteps of ancient, long-dead soldiers.[3] The Codori House interior, however, is off-limits to investigators since it is owned by the National Park Service.

Dozens of regiments—nearly 12,500 men—crossed the field of Pickett's Charge. After two days of stalemated combat, everyone involved with the charge knew of it's importance. Officers realized that it may have been the Confederacy's last chance to win a big victory on northern soil and go on to raid Harrisburg, capital of Pennsylvania, Philadelphia, or perhaps even Washington D.C., capital of the North. From mere private to the commanding general Robert E. Lee, emotions were running at an all-time high.

Not to mention the emotions in the Union Army, against whom the Confederates threw themselves. All involved believed that the outcome of the battle could hinge on the outcome of the charge; most knew that with a battle this far north, the outcome of the war might depend upon the charge; some who had the presence of mind to take logic to its end, may have even realized that upon the success or failure of Pickett's Charge depended the future of the United States in the world.

One thing is sure: every single person on either side knew that, as Pickett's Charge began to advance across the open fields, the next few minutes could possibly be their last on earth.

Each individual knew that in mere moments he could be in Heaven or Hell.

If those reasons are not enough to raise human emotions to an all-time high, I cannot think of a time or a place where they could be higher.

And, in just fifty minutes of battle, all those conflicts were resolved.

How to Get There

The field of Pickett's Charge is most easily accessed from the Confederate side of the battlefield. From Baltimore Street in Gettysburg, follow West Middle Street (Route 116 West) out of Gettysburg. At the top of the hill, turn left at the light at West Confederate Avenue. Follow West Confederate until you reach the Virginia Memorial on the left. Turn left and park in the lot. The woods ahead of you are the "Point of Woods;" the macadam pathway is just past the interpretive signs.

Tips on Investigating

Dusk is always a good time to visit the field of Pickett's Charge. So is the anniversary of the charge: July 3. The National Park Service has cut pathways in the crops in the huge field so that visitors may walk from the Virginia Monument all the way to the stone wall on the Union side of the field. Remember though, if you begin to walk at dusk, you may be returning after dark—not a recommended practice.

But people have reported paranormal experiences in broad daylight as well.

Begin at the Virginia Memorial and walk out the macadam path to the audio station. On your right will be the "Point of Woods." At the end of the macadam path you will see the cleared pathway through the crops. Follow that to the Emmitsburg Road.

WARNING! The Emmitsburg Road is a busy highway and people are often looking at monuments as they drive along it. Cross with care!

If you are trying to get E.V.P., find a spot where there is no traffic or insect noise. Some units to address would be those from Virginia, North Carolina, and Tennessee, whose troops made up most of the assaulting column in the area you will cross. Once on the Union side, E.V.P. may be a little more difficult because of traffic. (Although, if you investigate in the late fall or winter, extraneous noise should not be a problem.) Northern troops at the "Angle" came from Pennsylvania, New York, Connecticut, and Delaware.

For investigation purposes, let us use Armistead's Virginia Brigade (the 9th, 14th, 38th, 53rd, 57th Virginia Regiments). Armistead's men crossed the entire field of Pickett's Charge and followed their commander right up to the stone wall, the defensive position of the Union Army's Second Corps. Some of Armistead's men actually pierced the center of the Union line behind their commander as he leapt the wall shouting, "Give them the cold steel, boys! Who will follow me?"

Lewis Addison Armistead was born in New Bern, North Carolina, and attended West Point (but did not graduate).

Armistead's Brigade was mostly recruited from the area of Virginia south and east of Petersburg. The men of the 9th Virginia came from the Isle of Wight, Dinwiddie County, and Portsmouth, and were commanded by Colonel John C. Owens who was mortally wounded in Pickett's Charge. The 14th Virginia was mostly recruited from Amelia County, Liberty (now Bedford) County, Fluvanna County, Chesterfield County, Mecklenburg County, and Halifax County. Their commander, Colonel James G. Hodges, was killed during the charge. The 38th Virginia contained men from Halifax, Mecklenburg, but mostly Pittsylvania County.

Using names of home counties and of individuals may help facilitate your investigation. Calling on these individuals and mentioning their home counties, regimental numbers, or relatives' names seems to facilitate E.V.P. "Men of Pittsylvania County, are you here?" Using the original name for "Liberty" (now Bedford) County may help as well, since it has not been heard in decades.[4]

Armistead Monument

GENERAL ROBERT E. LEE'S HEADQUARTERS

The widow Thompson's stone house, adjacent to Larson's Quality Inn, was used as a temporary headquarters for Confederate commanding general Robert E. Lee. He took some meals there and a number of his officers met with him to discuss strategies. He also maintained headquarters' tents across the Chambersburg Pike. Both places would be areas of high emotional intensity, for decisions made there would alter American and World history. In fact, a number of unexplainable events in and around the grounds have confirmed that the paranormal has taken place there.

A guide for the *Ghosts of Gettysburg Candlelight Walking Tours*® was standing in the parking lot on the south side of Route 30 across from the Thompson House and overlooking the site of Lee's headquarters' tents. She had just finished telling her tale of a soldier buried alive under a pile of rotting corpses, discovered by surgeons too late to save him from a crazed, ranting death. As she finished, one of her guests pointed to the dark line of Reynolds' Woods from which Confederate soldiers had emerged some 138 years before. "Is that part of the tour?" he asked.

As the entire tour watched, a line of flashing lights sparkled from the woods.

"No," the guide replied. "We never set up fake 'ghosts.' Besides, that's National Park property. No one should be over there. Certainly no reenactment group this close to closing the park."

And yet, from somewhere out of time, what appeared to be a line of Civil War era infantry fired one last volley from the woods where they once struggled for the freedom of their new nation.[5]

In the Thompson House, now a museum commemorating the hours Robert E. Lee and his generals planned the battle before them, the psychic, Karyol Kirkpatrick, felt that four "major generals" sat and planned tactics for the fighting around Devil's Den. She also felt that there was "a lot of confusion...it seems as though one of the generals was not happy with what was going to take place." She referred, of course, to General James Longstreet's reluctance to wage Lee's battle of aggressive tactics, rather than the battle of maneuver he would have fought.

Without a doubt, large amounts of psychic energy—from Robert E. Lee knowing what was at stake here at Gettysburg, to Longstreet's reluctance to carry out Lee's orders—has embedded itself into the simple stone walls of the Thompson House.[6]

How to Get There

From Lincoln Square in Gettysburg, follow Route 30 West to the top of Seminary Ridge. Lee's Headquarters is on the right and well marked.

Tips on Investigating

Lee's Headquarters is a museum open to the public. There is a charge to enter. Since there may be groups of people in the house while you are there, use that to your advantage. I have found that when large groups enter an allegedly haunted area, they seem to stir up the entities and drive them away. However, as soon as the group leaves the room, out come the entities. Wait until the people have left the room, then try to take pictures and see what develops. Recording E.V.P., unless there is no one in the building, may be difficult, but worth a try.

REYNOLDS' WOODS

It was an unremarkable cluster of woods just south of the McPherson's Farmstead when the sun set on it June 30, 1863. It would later be named after one who never owned it, but paid for it with the dearest coin imaginable: his life.

Reynolds' Woods

The next morning, July 1, 1863, John Fulton Reynolds, native Pennsylvanian, Major General and commander of the Union Army's First Corps, was at the apex of his career and power. He had been offered the command of the entire Union Army not long before, but turned it down: he was a fighting soldier, not a political one and did not want to get embroiled in that mess. So, instead of being entangled in lines of communication to Washington and buried in paperwork at the rear, he rode at the very head of his column of marching men, across the ripe fields of his native state, through the Lutheran Seminary, toward the damp mustiness of this dark woods just before him. He must have felt an incredible swell of pride as he turned in his saddle to watch his men fan out into their lines of battle. It was the last thing on earth he would ever see.

A Confederate minie ball struck him high in the back of his neck, shattering whatever vision he might have been witnessing. All glory, all power, all vanity was washed away in a split second, and John Reynolds would be seen no more upon this earth.

Or some would say.

Aides would carry his body back through the seminary, along a path that would someday be covered, as the school grew, with modern dormitories for aspiring men and women of the cloth. It seems that along the route of this last journey, the General has passed again.

A seminarian was awakened one night by a scream piercing the dormitory hall. Recognizing the voice of a friend, he assumed there was some fooling around and so fell back asleep. About an hour later, he was awakened by a chill in his room. He opened his eyes to see a man—or rather, half a man—the top half—standing, darkly glowering in his very room. He stood to confront the intruder, and the dark, bearded man vanished before his eyes.

Along the edge of the woods that faces the town, there seems to be some strange activity. From the road that runs through the Seminary, on certain nights can be seen what some parapsychologists call a "Warp," or "Tear," in the veil of Time. Out of place, out of all worldly order, from the edge of the woods will be seen that strange, flashing line of lights, the color ranging from light to navy blue. They light up as if "firing at will" from one end of the line to the other, a re-creation of what happened there some fourteen decades past, but in the hue more associated with the supernatural than historical fact.

How to Get There

To see Reynolds' Woods from the Lutheran Seminary: From Lincoln Square in Gettysburg, follow Route 30 West to the top of Seminary Ridge (at Lee's Headquarters.) Turn left onto the Seminary Road. Park in the appropriate spaces and look to the west at Reynolds' Woods.

To get to Reynolds' Woods, continue on Route 30 West past Lee's Headquarters and through the light on Route 30 West. Turn left at the road just past the stone-ended McPherson Barn and follow the road around to the east edge of the woods where Reynolds was killed.

Tips on Investigating

The Reynolds' Woods area is nearly always busy and noisy, so E.V.P. may be out of the question. Photos may work in the woods, especially early in the morning or at dusk. General Reynolds' sweetheart was named Kate Hewitt. No one, not even Reynolds' family apparently, knew about her and was surprised when she came to the viewing of his body in nearby Lancaster, Pennsylvania. She was so heartbroken by her betrothed's death that she joined the convent in nearby Emmitsburg, Maryland. Reynolds' faithful aide's name was Charles Veil, who literally caught the General as he slipped from his horse after being shot. Those are both names you may want to try in your investigation.[7]

WARNING! The Lutheran Theological Seminary is a private institution. Please respect the privacy of the students and faculty who live in the houses and dormitories there. Be reminded to verify the closing time for the National Park Service roads.

HAUNTED SITES ON THE SOUTH END OF THE BATTLEFIELD

DEVIL'S DEN AND THE SLAUGHTER PEN

Actually, Devil's Den's haunted areas consist of two separate sites: Devil's Den itself, the familiar jumble of huge boulders across from the parking lot as one enters the area, and the Slaughter Pen, the area across Plum Run from the parking area. (The Triangular Field is also part of the complex, but is so active that it will be covered in a separate section.)

One of the first ghost stories told about Devil's Den pre-dates the great battle for the unique jumble of boulders which, during the fighting, became slick with the blood that pooled in the depressions in the rocks.

It is the story of two hunters who were lost in the area. Before the battlefield roads were constructed, it is easy to see how someone could get lost in the maze of house-sized boulders. The hunters apparently had wandered around for a while, backtracking and running into dead ends in the labyrinth of giant rocks. It began growing cold and dark. Unless they got out they would have to spend the night in the eerie place. Suddenly they spotted what appeared to be another human. No description remains of his attire, but it must have been something compelling to the hunters. He signaled for the men to follow, which they did at a distance. They suddenly found themselves in a familiar area where they could find their way out of Devil's Den. When they tried to catch up to thank the stranger who led them to safety, he simply vanished before their eyes.

Other stories recount an apparently helpful—and talkative—Confederate soldier who appeared out of nowhere to tell a lost young lady that, "what you are looking for is over there." She turned to see what he was pointing at, realized that he could not have known 'what she was looking for,' and just as quickly turned back, only to see that he was gone in a flash. She described his uniform to a park ranger: ragged, unkempt, floppy hat, barefoot, and the ranger realized she was describing the outfit of a Texas soldier, who, by coincidence (if you believe in coincidence) were the very soldiers who fought their way through Devil's Den.[1] This, of course, is an example of what Joshua Warren identifies as an "Entity," or a spirit that interacts with the living.

Visitors have reported the sound of muffled singing floating through the Den and apparently coming from the dark, wooded side of Big Round Top. The odd part is that the songs heard are decidedly Southern in nature. Military bugles, drums, hoarse shouts of an entire regiment of men, cannon-fire, and rolls of faint musketry are also heard from the area, wafting strangely through Devil's Den. Bagpipes, too, have been heard. In the 1960's, one woman claimed to have had her ankle grabbed when she slipped into a crack in one of the boulders in Devil's Den. Both she and her friend, when they looked to see what had grabbed her, saw in the crevice a ragged Confederate soldier.[2]

Devil's Den

Some of the men who were killed at Devil's Den fell into the huge fissures in the rocks, or were purposely thrown into the crevices, when fellow soldiers realized they could not dig graves in the rocky area. There is that theory in paranormal studies which attributes the lingering of spirits to quartz infused rocks, such as those abundant in Devil's Den and throughout the Gettysburg area. (See previous chapter, "Gettysburg: The Paranormal Experience.") Some scientific studies say the 100 billion brain cells in humans produce enough electricity, while we are thinking, to light an incandescent bulb. Creating electricity also creates electromagnetic waves which, so researchers postulate, can be caught by the quartz in granite rock. It is captured and replayed in numerous manifestations—audible, tactile, visual—upon certain occasions.

Certainly, during the time of the battle for Devil's Den and imminent sudden death of the soldiers fighting among the rocks, their brains were working as hard as they could trying to figure out a way to survive, or desperately contemplating their own sudden extinction.

THE SLAUGHTER PEN

As you stand in the parking lot, turn to your left. Confederate attacks pushed through the "Plum Run Gorge," the area between Devil's Den on the left and the Slaughter Pen and Little Round Top on the right. It was in this area that, true to his premonition given to friends that he would be killed, Lieutenant Colonel William T. Harris, commander of the 2nd Georgia, fell. The fighting in the area ahead of you was so vicious that it received the name "Valley of Death."

How to Get There

To Devil's Den: From Lincoln Square in Gettysburg, head south on Baltimore Street and follow the signs for Route 15 South (the Emmitsburg Road.) At the first crossroads (The Peach Orchard) turn left. Follow this into the valley and turn right onto Crawford Avenue. At the stop sign go straight. The parking lot for Devil's Den is on the left.

To the Slaughter Pen from Devil's Den: Walk across the bridge from the Devil's Den parking lot towards the restrooms. To the left is a pathway that leads into the Slaughter Pen and the Valley of Death. The path to the right takes you through the woods along Plum Run. Perhaps it is this proximity to water, as some paranormalists theorize, that makes this area susceptible to hauntings. Turn right to follow the pathway across Plum Run and to the bottom of the Triangular Field.

WARNING! Explore with care! Rugged terrain ahead. This area is _not_ recommended for investigation after dark.

The farther down the path you get, the more rugged the terrain gets until you have to cross Plum Run, also known as "Bloody Run," since it was tainted red by the blood of the men who fought in the valley it drains—the "Valley of Death." If you continue along the path you will eventually come to the bottom of the slope of the Triangular Field.

Strange photos with what appear to be faces have been captured on this pathway. One group of college students playing with a Ouija Board called forth a ghostly, glowing Civil War soldier and his lady from the woods behind the restroom building.[3]

Tips on Investigating

The 1st Texas Regiment of Hood's Division, along with men from the 2nd and 17th Georgia Infantry, were the soldiers who fought so hard for possession of Devil's Den against men from the 99th Pennsylvania, the 4th Maine, the 40th

New York Infantry, and Smith's Battery of Artillery. The 44th Alabama fought through the Slaughter Pen.

If you are using a recorder to attempt to capture E.V.P., try addressing Hood's Texans. Be respectful. Remember, you are intruding into *their* world. Be sure to pause at least 40 seconds between questions if you are using a voice activated recorder.

If you are videotaping or trying still shots and you have an electromagnetic field meter or remote temperature sensor, find likely spots with those first, then take a photo or video.

THE TRIANGULAR FIELD

Cameras seem to malfunction more in this field than anywhere else on the battlefield, or in the town of Gettysburg. Everything from point-and-click disposables to television cameras costing tens of thousands of dollars have been affected. It is almost as if whatever spirits reside there are angry at photographers.[4] Countless other still and video cameras have malfunctioned just within the boundaries of the field, after they had worked perfectly *outside* the confines of the field.

The Triangular Field

Confederate units such as the 15th, 20th, and 17th Georgia, and 1st Texas attacked up the slope towards Smith's Battery at the top of the Triangular Field. Counterattacks were made by the 124th New York—the famous "Orange Blossoms" of Orange County, New York. Major James Cromwell of the 124th New York led the charge and was killed by a shot in the chest and fell backwards off his horse. Colonel A. Van Horne Ellis, commander of the 124th New York, saw him go down, charged into the fray, and was shot in the head, plunging forward off his horse headfirst into the rocks, a dead man. The bodies of Ellis and Cromwell were placed upon a rock in the rear of the line of the 124th. Other Union officers who were killed in the oddly-shaped field from the 124th New York were Captain Isaac Nichols of Company G, wedged between two rocks, and the two unidentified men who tried to save his body from the enemy. Company I lost Lieutenant Milnor Brown, a newcomer to the unit, killed among strangers.

At the top of the Triangular Field stood four guns of Smith's Battery. Like some sort of deadly game of "capture the flag," a number of men from the 1st Texas sacrificed their lives just to get near or climb upon the abandoned guns. One private and a comrade got to the guns as a shell exploded, blasting a hole in one of the men's chest the size of a fist. He staggered around for five minutes, then died. Corporal William A. Duvall laid a hand on a cannon and was shot down. Private E. P. Derrick positioned himself behind a large boulder alongside his Captain, George T. Todd. One of the huge .58 caliber minie balls smashed into the unlucky private's head, blowing his blood and brains into his Captain's face. Colonel John A. Jones, commander of the 20th Georgia, lay on his back in the field in front of Smith's guns, half of his head removed by the fragment of a cannon shell.[5]

How to Get There

The Triangular Field can be reached either on foot via the pathway from the Slaughter Pen, or by car. To drive there, continue up through Devil's Den. As the road levels out, cannons representing Smith's Battery will be on your right. A parking pull-off will be on the right near some National Park Service interpretive signs. Park and walk across the road. The Triangular Field is ahead inside the gate at the stone wall.

Tips on Investigating

If you wish to try to gather E.V.P., names of men from the 15th Georgia are available in the appendix of my book, *35 Days to Gettysburg: The Campaign Diaries of Two American Enemies*. I had success calling the men of the 15th Georgia to attention, then reading their names as in a roll call. All photos or video should be backed up, if possible, by documentation with scientific equipment, such as electromagnetic field sensors or remote thermal scanners.

LITTLE ROUND TOP

There was little activity on Little Round Top during the morning and early afternoon of July 2, 1863. In fact, no one seemed to even know the name of the small, cleared, rocky hill lying in the shadow of a much larger hill to its south. On the eminence there were a few signalmen and the Federals' chief engineering officer, Major General Gouverneur K. Warren, sent by the Union Army commander to see what was going on there. After analyzing the Union line, which was stretched out to the north, he realized that the hill he was on was the key to the entire Union position—should the Confederates take it, they would have access to the flank and rear of his army and could force a Union retreat from Gettysburg. There were thick woods on Big Round Top and on the ridges behind Devil's Den that would make fine cover for an advancing enemy, hiding them until the last minute of an assault. With no idea just where the Confederates were, Warren was apprehensive. Having been in command of infantry before he became chief engineer, he knew foot soldiers well. He ordered a section of Smith's Battery of artillery in the valley below to lob a shell into the woods. As the shell crashed into the trees, Warren was amazed to see a long, glistening line sparkling in the shadows—the reflection of sunlight off thousands of musket barrels and bayonets as Confederates, standing in the woods, flinched and turned to avoid the artillery shell.

From this Warren knew the enemy was only moments away from taking the hill, so he sent for the nearest friendly troops. Colonel Strong Vincent's Brigade responded and, in wrapping his brigade around the south and west slope of Little Round Top, placed the 20th Maine, commanded by Colonel Joshua Chamberlain, at the extreme left of the entire Army of the Potomac. Soon the dying would begin.

The fight for Little Round Top was fierce as the opposing lines see-sawed back and forth, up and down the slope, while Lieutenant Charles E. Hazlett's Battery D, Fifth U. S. Artillery, boomed above and behind them. Young Hazlett had a premonition that this would be his last fight. Brigadier General Stephen Weed was shot near the summit of Little Round Top. As Hazlett bent over Weed to receive a last message, the premonition came true. A Confederate bullet pierced his skull.

Twenty-six year old Vincent would be mortally wounded too, suffering for five days before succumbing to his wounds.

Charles Hazlett was not the only one fighting for Little Round Top whose premonition of death came true. Captain Lucius S. Larrabee, Company B, 44th New York Regiment, told friends that he would be killed the very next time they engaged the enemy. So convinced was he of his impending demise that he gave his valuables away and said good-bye to his comrades, even though the war had spared every officer in the regiment thus far. Larrabee led

Company B forward on the skirmish line between the slope of Little Round Top and Big Round Top. They found some Texans, fired at them and began to retreat. For a while it looked as if Larrabee was safe. Then, an enemy minie ball passed through him and he fell, victim of some unknown Confederate, and fate.

Colonel Joshua L. Chamberlain and the 20th Maine held the extreme left flank of the Union line. At the very beginning of the fight a sergeant from Company A, Charles Steele, was shot in the chest. "I am going, Captain," he said to his commanding officer and fell dying.

Little Round Top

On the Confederate side attacking Chamberlain was the 15th Alabama led by Colonel William C. Oates. Oates' brother, John Oates, was a lieutenant with the regiment and was ill that day. The Colonel told him he did not have to advance, but John was stung by the suggestion and said he would not have people think he was a coward. He would attack with the regiment, unless he were killed, which he thought likely. Colonel Oates last saw his brother alive, leading the men toward the Union line, when puffs of dust suddenly appeared from the Lieutenant's coat—numerous bullets striking him all at once—and he fell.

While the battle raged, Oates shouted an order to Captain James Ellison and watched as Ellison began to lead his troops forward. Suddenly, Oates saw a bullet strike Ellison in the head. Ellison fell on his side and in spite of the bullet in his brain, still struggled for life: he rolled over on his back, lifted his arms over his head, clenched his fists, shuddered, and died.[6]

Colonel Patrick O'Rorke of the 140th New York would not allow his men to fire until they were within forty feet of the Confederates on the west slope of Little Round Top. His men got into line with the other regiments of Vincent's Brigade and "Paddy" O'Rorke gave the order to fire. One unlucky Confederate shot O'Rorke through the neck; return fire from the lead companies of the 140th put some seventeen bullets into O'Rorke's killer.

How to Get There

From the town of Gettysburg, head south on the Emmitsburg Road. At the first crossroads (The Peach Orchard) turn left. Follow this into the valley and turn right onto Crawford Avenue. At the stop sign turn left. At the next stop sign turn left. Follow the road to the parking areas on Little Round Top. To get to the marker of the 20th Maine, walk back down the road you came up and bear left at the pathway halfway down. Markers and the pathway will lead you to the monument.

Tips on Investigating

Vincent's wounding site is marked halfway down the southern slope near the road. Regimental markers for the 20th Maine, 140th New York (where O'Rorke fell), and the rest of Vincent's Brigade ring the south and west slopes of Little Round Top. Oates' 15th Alabama fought through the southern "saddle" between Little Round Top and the north slope of Big Round Top and curled their way around the back of Little Round Top. Most of their casualties occurred there.

For days after the battle on Little Round Top, the dead and wounded from both sides lay scattered along the west slope, the small valley between Little Round Top and Big Round Top to the south, and along the summit. Nearly anywhere you walk along the fabled hill you pass through a space where some Union or Confederate soldier spent his last seconds on earth, or was traumatically wounded. Specifically, if you climb to the very summit of Little Round Top, between Hazlett's cannons, you will see a flat rock with a faded, worn inscription on it. It was on this rock that General Weed fell, and where Hazlett bent over him for some whispered word, and was shot dead upon the body of his commander. This may be a good place to attempt still camera shots or E.V.P. at dusk.

If you walk back down the hill along the road, opposite the direction you drove up, you will see a small pathway leading into the woods on the left. Follow this pathway, past the stone wall that marks the battle line of the 20th Maine. The path ends at the monument to the regiment. Because of the motion picture "Gettysburg," most times of the year the area is crowded and so, while good E.V.P. and orb photographs have been captured here, it is usually too active with the living to be able to successfully contact the dead.

Stone Marking the Mortal Wounding of Weed and Hazlett

However, if you continue down the road and bear to the left, through the small parking lot, and turn to the left along a less-used, flat path that seems to bend back north, you will be in an area that is hardly visited and a potential site for investigation. This dirt road running behind the eastern side of Little Round Top was once known as Chamberlain Avenue. According to Captain Porter Farley of the 140th New York, 26 men of the regiment were killed in the action that saved Little Round Top for the Union: "Grouped by companies, a row of inanimate forms lay side by side beneath the trees upon this eastern slope. No funeral ceremony, and only shallow graves could be accorded them. In the darkness of the night, silently and with bitter dejection, each Company buried its dead."[7]

Chamberlain Avenue

Joshua Chamberlain, in his official report of the battle, also mentions returning to Little Round Top on July 4 and burying some of the men of the 20th Maine "in the place where we had laid them during the fight," probably behind their lines, definitely on Little Round Top, near where you are standing. They also buried fifty of the enemy's dead "In front of our position of July 2." This was confirmed by a newspaper correspondent from Philadelphia.[8] The Union men buried on the eastern side of Little Round Top were probably exhumed within a few months to be re-interred in the National Cemetery. The Confederates, sadly, remained buried until the early 1870's, when they were probably exhumed and sent to Southern cemeteries.

In other words, the area to the south and east of the 20th Maine marker was a temporary burial ground.

ROSE WOODS AND ROSE FARM

WARNING! While most of the historic houses on the battlefield are public property, they are often occupied by park rangers. Do not disturb the residents! Do not attempt an investigation around a house after the posted Park visitation hours!

In late June, 1863, John Rose and his wife Anna prepared for the summer growing season. Most, if not all of their crops would have been in, and the waist-high wheat in their large wheatfield would be approaching reaping time. To help them was Francis Ogden and his wife, who lived in the large stone house with the Rose's. It must have been rather crowded, as well, for the two families had fourteen children between them. One can only imagine the children, as friendly as brothers and sisters, frolicking in the fields around the farm.

Rose Farm

But perhaps there was more than just friendship—at least between two of the children.

Mary Josephine Rose was nearing twenty years old in 1863; Charles Francis Ogden was approaching the age of marriage as well. If there ever was a romantic relationship between these two of the same age, who had grown up together, who played and worked in the same fields together, we may never know. Charles, following his patriot's heart, joined the Union army in August of 1862 and fought with the 138th Pennsylvania.

When the battle in her own dooryard was over, Mary Josephine was exposed to things unthinkable to proper Victorian young ladies. No doubt, as she helped clean the gore from her parents' home, and watched from her bedroom windows as soldiers were unceremoniously buried in mass graves, she wondered if her childhood friend Charles Ogden was among them.

Perhaps by November she had happily discovered that Charles had not been among the dead at Gettysburg. But her joy was tempered. Outside her kitchen door exhumations had begun, and the now decomposed remains of the Union soldiers were dragged from their graves and taken to the new National Cemetery on Cemetery Hill in Gettysburg.

Then the blow came. Charles Ogden had indeed escaped the bloody hell that was Gettysburg only to be killed in another battle. Mary Josephine Rose's horror was total. What she saw happen to the unfamiliar soldiers out in her yard had happened to her lifelong companion, Charles, in a different place.

But that was apparently not enough. Sometime in 1871, a local doctor, Rufus Weaver, began to have crews exhume the Confederates who were buried on the farm. This horror was even more acute, for after some eight years in the ground, without proper embalming, the remains of the Southerners were appalling.

In the Daybook of local Gettysburg doctor J. W. C. O'Neil there are several entries referring to having to visit the Rose farmhouse and treat one of the women. The final entry intimates that he had to restrain her by means of a straight jacket. . .

The Rose Farm represents one of the larger burial sites, and one of the bloodiest battlegrounds, at Gettysburg. J. Howard Wert, a visitor to the battlefield shortly after the end of the fighting, wrote that graves were all around the house, barn, and outbuildings with 10 Confederate graves clustered behind the house and 175 behind the Rose barn. (Another visitor to the farm counted 275.) Wert also stated that there was a rebel colonel buried within a yard of Mrs. Rose's kitchen door. And another observer counted, in the Rose garden, almost 100 Confederates in shallow graves.

The Rose Farm was one of the first battle sites discovered by photographers coming up from Washington via Emmitsburg, Maryland, on July 5, 1863. Anyone driving north along the Emmitsburg Road can see the same terrain features famed Civil War photographer Alexander Gardner and his assistants saw: The Rose farmhouse, the Rose Woods and the undulating terrain that was once spotted with strange dark outcroppings which, upon approach, could be identified as dead men's bodies.

One minute you are striding alongside your comrades, emotions piqued to a fevered pitch, anticipating the clash with the enemy. Suddenly, there they are, standing with rifles pointed at you. From their muskets comes a flash of fire and before you can hear the discharge, you are struck by an ounce of lead, flying at 900 feet per second. The result is like an electric shock to your body: arms go weak and you drop your musket; in spite of your brain protesting, your legs grow limp and wobbly and you drop uncontrollably, knee to a sharp rock, bumping into a comrade, head hitting the parched ground. If you are able, if the bullet has not paralyzed you or rendered you unconscious, you roll over and somehow find the strength to look for your wound. You find a ragged hole in your butternut-colored jacket the size of your thumb that also goes through your wool vest. Now you are frantic: somehow you find the strength to rip open your vest and shirt and see a bloody hole just above your belt. As you watch, blood begins to pump from the wound. You reach around to your back and find a hole the size of your fist and the world around you begins to go hazy and dark. You try to think but you realize there is nothing you can do; hope is moving out of your mind and all you can think about is your wife, your children. . .your home. . .your mother. . .

How to Get There

From the town of Gettysburg, head south on the Emmitsburg Road. At the first crossroads (The Peach Orchard) turn left. Follow this into the valley and turn right onto Crawford Avenue. At the stop sign go straight. Follow the road through Devil's Den and the Triangular Field area. (It is one-way.) Turn left at the first crossroads. You will be on Cross Avenue. That will become Brooke Avenue and you will soon see the National Park Service plaques on the left. View the National Park Service plaques and you can see the area as it looked at the time of the battle through the camera lens of Alexander Gardner.

Tips for Investigating

The Rose Farm and the area you will be traveling through was fought over by nearly 20,500 men for about five hours on July 2, 1863. Some of the units lost 33 to 37 percent of their troops in casualties during those five hours. The dead, dying, and wounded—Union and Confederate alike—lay all around where you are standing. Confederate units that marched and died at the Rose farm were predominantly from Kershaw's South Carolina Brigade. The left wing of Kershaw's Brigade halted near the barn to re-align their ranks, shifted to the left and advanced toward Union artillery batteries and infantry in the Peach Orchard. In this vicinity, Captain Robert C. Pulliam was killed. One of Kershaw's regiments passed between the house and barn and the other advanced around the house.

Union troops who fought against them to the east of the farm were from Pennsylvania, Massachusetts, and Michigan. Private Charles Phillips, of the 22nd Michigan, became one of the first casualties when a bullet smashed into his head. Private John Morrison, also of the 22nd, true to a premonition he had on the march to Gettysburg, took a bullet in the belly, and died later.[9]

THE WHEATFIELD

The Wheatfield can be a very good area for investigation for a number of reasons. It is easily located from several roads; it is in the middle of the battlefield and therefore relatively quiet; and it is a fairly large field where an investigator can stand in the middle and hardly be disturbed by extraneous sounds and human activity. As well, and sadly, it was the scene of one of the bloodiest and most violent conflicts in the Battle of Gettysburg.[10]

The Wheatfield

The 61st New York Regiment lost 60 percent of its men in the fighting. The unit was recruited from Staten Island and their monument is visible in the Wheatfield. A walk to the monument and reference to their place of organization may aid in your investigation.

Also plainly visible in the field is the monument to the 27th Connecticut with an eagle prominent on top. Lieutenant Colonel Henry C. Merwin of the 27th was mortally wounded near this monument.

Closer to the Wheatfield Road is a stone shaft standing on a large rock. It was in this vicinity that Brigadier General Samuel K. Zook was shot in the stomach and mortally wounded. Zook was a native Pennsylvanian, raised in the eastern part of the state very near the Revolutionary War site of Valley

Forge. He had been wounded at Fredericksburg in December of 1862, and fought at the Battle of Chancellorsville in May of 1863.

To the right, a little farther down the Wheatfield Road, is where a strange and deadly premonition came true. Colonel Edward E. Cross, commanding a brigade of New York, New Hampshire, and Pennsylvania troops, had a premonition just before the battle. To an aide on June 28, he assigned the duty of caring for his trunk of belongings, saying he would not make it through the next battle—wherever that might be. The aide tried to laugh it off, but Cross was morbidly serious. Just before advancing into the maelstrom that was the Wheatfield on July 2, he had the aide tie his customary silk bandana around his head. The aide was shocked to discover that Cross had replaced his usual red scarf with a black one. As he led his men toward the Wheatfield, Cross was met by his Corps commander, Major General Winfield Hancock, who said, "Cross, this is the last battle you'll fight without a star," meaning that Hancock was going to promote the Colonel to brigadier general after Gettysburg. "Sorry, General," Cross replied. "This is my last battle."

When his line halted for a moment, Cross stepped out in front of the 5th New Hampshire to reconnoiter the ground ahead. For a Confederate hidden behind a large rock the shot at a Yankee colonel, only about fifty yards away, was too tempting. He put a bullet into Cross' belly, mortally wounding him. The Confederate's glee at taking out an officer was short-lived: the smoke and flash revealed his position and the commander of the 5th ordered a sergeant to pick off the man. The next time he exposed himself, the rebel sharpshooter was shot. Revenge too, was brief. Within a few hours, the sergeant was killed. The boulder is in the southwest corner of Brooke and Sickles Avenues.

How to Get There

From Devil's Den: Continue up through Devil's Den. As the road levels out, cannons representing Smith's Battery will be on your right. (If you wish to visit the Triangular Field, park in the parking spaces ahead on the right and follow directions in the Triangular Field Section of this book.) Continue along the road until you see the sign for The Wheatfield on your right.

From the Rose Farm plaques: Continue along Brooke Avenue to the stop sign. Ahead of you is The Wheatfield.

From the Town of Gettysburg: Head south on Business Route 15. Turn left on the Wheatfield Road and follow down the long hill into the valley. You will see a sign identifying The Wheatfield and begin to see monuments on your right starting with a shaft monument to Brigadier General Zook.

Tips on Investigating

Once again, try to relate with those noble souls who gave so much for their country by referring to their home states, or perhaps, with a specifically named individual. Remember to pause at least forty seconds when trying E.V.P. and to always be respectful.

HAUNTED SITES IN THE TOWN OF GETTYSBURG

Many believe that the Federal Government, in the form of the National Park, owns the entire battlefield of Gettysburg and, therefore, any ghost investigations must conclude when the park closes.

The town of Gettysburg, however, is open all night (provided you are older than the curfew age of eighteen). The town boasts of even *more* historic structures than are on the National Park, and there are many places that can be accessed without disturbing the townsfolk.

Before attempting to do an investigation of the town of Gettysburg, it is recommended that you take one or more of the *Ghosts of Gettysburg Candlelight Walking Tours®* to familiarize yourself with the more haunted sites in town. Knowledgeable guides escort you on tours of different areas of the town. They are also privy to which areas have been most active recently. Another option would be to purchase one or more of the *Ghosts of Gettysburg* books, which have maps on their back covers to lead you to many of the haunted sites discussed in this book.

GHOSTS OF GETTYSBURG HEADQUARTERS:
271 BALTIMORE STREET

The *Ghosts of Gettysburg Candlelight Walking Tours®* purchased the property at 271 Baltimore Street in 1997. It is the center for Ghost Tours in Gettysburg. Like many of the historic structures in town, it was built in stages. In 1834, a small building containing a carriage trimmer's shop appears on the tax rolls for the site. In 1837, Jacob Heck was taxed 2.6 times that much for improvements on his property, indicating the construction of the two-story brick section that fronts Breckenridge Street. This date makes it one of the older structures in the borough of Gettysburg.

On September 24, 1849, Andrew Woods, a carriage trimmer and dealer, and his wife Sarah, purchased the property and owned it through the years which included the Battle of Gettysburg. The next increase in tax assessment does not appear until 1888, which would correspond with the construction of the section that faces Baltimore Street.

On July 2, 1863, the house became part of the Confederate battle lines which stretched through the town. According to historian Elwood Christ, "The second story of the house afforded sharpshooters a vantage point from which to harass Federal troops in the vicinity of the Rupp Tannery and along the Emmitsburg Road towards the Dobbin House." Historian Christ also reported that the Henry Comfort house, immediately to the north, and the James Pierce house, across Breckenridge Street on the corner, both became temporary field hospitals, which would indicate that the Andrew Woods house saw its share of wounded and dead in and around the structure as well.

The Ghosts of Gettysburg Tour Headquarters

Leonard Marsden Gardner wrote *Sunset Memories: A Retrospect of a Life lived during the last Seventy Five Years of the Nineteenth Century 1831-1901.* In it he described Baltimore Street as it appeared on Sunday, July 5, 1863, two days after the fighting ended:

"The wounded had been removed but the dead lay unburied and the ground was strewn with abandoned muskets, knapsacks, canteens and other accoutrements of war. The houses were marked with shot and shell on both sides of the street. Some with ugly gaps in the wall and others with a well defined hole where the cannon ball entered. A frame building particularly attracted my attention. It stood in a position facing the Union front and the weather boarding from top to within a few feet of the ground was literally honey-combed with the Minie balls. No boards were torn or displaced but thousands of neat round holes marked the places where the balls entered."

Gardner continues his narrative, specifically describing the corner upon which "The Ghost House" stands:

"Passing on I came to the point where Breckenridge Street connects with Baltimore. There a barricade was throw across the street. Through an opening at one end I led my horse and remounting I rode on down the street. A few persons only could be seen on the pavements. A scene of desolation and death was presented all the way. The unburied dead and the mangled remains of human bodies, mingled with debris of broken gun carriages, muskets, bayonets, and swords, which lay around in confusion on that lonely street in the quiet Sabbath morning, was one of those pictures of desolation which will never fade from my mind."

On March 26, 1866, Woods sold the house and lot to a cobbler, David Kitzmiller, and his wife, for $1,000 cash. The Kitzmillers owned the house for 26 years. When they moved into the house, they brought with them at least one child, Charles B. Kitzmiller. At least two Kitzmiller children—Eva Jane and William Henry—were born in the house. Sadly, at least one Kitzmiller offspring associated with the house died: William Henry died on February 1, 1899, at 24 years of age.

There were perhaps more deaths in the house: A mysterious entry in the Kitzmiller genealogical record in the list of the children of David and Mary Ann states, "Babes–number unspecified." As well, while not giving a specific date of death, first-born George Edward was baptized just 12 days after his birth, indicating that his survival was in question. There is neither a death date nor burial site specified for George Edward, nor names, dates of birth or death, for the "Babes–number unspecified." They seem to just disappear from the records of the family and the house.

David Kitzmiller died in 1914, and upon Mary's death the house passed on to the surviving children who sold it out of the family.

But, though they have died, it seems as if some of the former residents are reluctant to leave. Numerous unexplainable activities have occurred within the confines of the house.

As you enter the house, you might be surprised. It certainly does not look like a "Ghost House." But in that first room a number of dark, unexplainable, paranormal events have occurred.

One quiet evening, employees at the *Ghosts of Gettysburg Candlelight Walking Tours*® heard footsteps lightly descend the stairs and stop at the bottom. Peering into the darkened hall, they saw no one. Two hours later, from the darkness at the bottom of the stairs, there materialized a small boy, age 6 or 7. Witnesses saw him clearly enough to describe him with dirty blonde hair, wearing a light shirt with dark pants and suspenders. He stood there, looking into the front room. Then, as suddenly as he had entered this world, he disappeared from it.

An employee was in the bathroom washing her hands when the small brass door handle began making the clicking and squeaking sound which accompanies its movement. She dried her hands within a second and turned the handle herself, expecting to see her co-worker standing in front of the door playing with the doorknob. *No one was there.* She walked the two or three steps into the main room to see her co-worker seated behind the desk.

A month later, it happened again. And it happened to yet a third employee: again the familiar squeak and rattle; as she looked to the small handle, it turned. Exiting the room revealed...*no one.*

When psychic Karyol Kirkpatrick toured the house, one of her impressions was that of a child whom she said had died upstairs. Indeed, there was even more recent evidence of a child spirit's playfulness in the very room where you stand to get your tickets.

An employee felt her sweater being pulled. Her co-worker, eyes wide with astonishment exclaimed, "I just saw the back of your sweater pull out all by itself!"

Walking through the small, arched doorway under the sign marked "To Tours" places you in the Civil War period section of the house. Erase in your mind the bookshelves, fan, and electric lights. Replace them all with gaslights or candles, perhaps some 19th Century furnishings and antique carpets. But make sure that some of the carpets are bloodstained. Place Confederate soldiers in the corners and leaning up against the walls, exhausted, dirty, perhaps bloody, smelling like sulfur (from the black powder they used in their weapons), sweat, and fear.

Karyol Kirkpatrick mentioned during her visit that she "saw injured persons and blood" and a couple of men hiding in the basement below your feet. She heard music and instruments. (It was common for fighting men of all eras to amuse themselves—when not fighting for their lives—with song and easily carried instruments like harmonicas.) She got the impression of men from Georgia and Virginia in the house. (Documentation proves that Georgians were the troops occupying this section of Gettysburg. Virginians may have straggled here from their lines on Long Lane just a few hundred yards to the west.) And, not surprisingly, she never mentioned Northern troops as being present.

Karyol saw a woman in dark clothing who "did not have it all together," but only as a ruse, so that no one paid her any attention. The woman had a mission as a secret courier. She mentioned a woman named "Mary" who loved cooking—Karyol smelled mince pie—and she "received" the name "James," and heard a man talking incessantly about God.

Once through the first room of the Civil War section, you enter into the second (of three) rooms. An associate of the *Ghosts of Gettysburg Candlelight*

Walking Tours® had just finished spending some time in that room. It was late at night and the building was closing for the evening. An unusually large number of customers had passed through that night since there had been a book signing. (Remember, researchers have discovered that in order to increase your chances of photographing spirit entities, you must first fill a room with people, then empty it. It seems as if the entities return, after a large crowd has left, to see what was going on. That is just what happened that night.) The associate was behind the exit door pushing it closed and had turned toward the far wall. He was alone in the room. . .but not for long.

Out of the corner of his eye he saw the figure of a small woman, seemingly cloaked in a long, dark, flowing dress with a wide-brimmed black hat. He stood for a brief moment, afraid to look directly at her, since entities can sometimes only be seen through peripheral vision. Indeed, when he turned to confront the dark lady, she vanished.[1]

How to Get There

From Lincoln Square, follow Baltimore Street south for three blocks. The *Ghosts of Gettysburg Candlelight Walking Tours*® Headquarters building is at 271 Baltimore Street, on the corner of Baltimore and Breckenridge Streets.

Tips on Investigating

It is always difficult to find a quiet time in the *Ghosts of Gettysburg* office, since customers can wander through the first floor of the building during business hours. There are, however, lulls during the day. If you are going to take pictures or try some E.V.P., please check in with the desk personnel and let them know what you are doing. Try calling on the former inhabitants of the house: Jacob Heck, Andrew and Sarah Woods, David and Mary Ann Kitzmiller, or their children Charles, Eva Jane, George Edward and William Henry.

GETTYSBURG COLLEGE

Those who study the paranormal almost universally credit high human energy levels with psychic activity. Teenage years, in particular, appear to create manifestations that seem to be emanating from the Otherworld. Poltergeist activity—"Noisy ghosts"—where unseen entities fling material items to and fro across rooms, or knock on walls, or bump things off shelves, has been attributed to emotional energy generated by teenagers. So it is no wonder then that Gettysburg College has its share of ghosts.

In 1837, Pennsylvania College moved from a building it shared with the Lutheran Seminary on High Street to Pennsylvania Hall, northwest of the town of Gettysburg. For years the small college went about its business of matriculating and graduating students, educating them in religion and mathematics and the sciences. The school enjoyed a genteel and measured existence in a peaceful, rural setting. Then, in July of 1863, it was suddenly witness to great quantities of human suffering during and after the Battle of Gettysburg.

Union troops, rushing headlong into the battle—and perhaps to their own demise as well—marched across the campus toward the fighting taking place in the fields just north of town. (The fields across which they moved are now playing fields for the college.) The men were filled with high emotions: of the anxiety of impending combat and the chance of being wounded or killed.

As soon as they began taking casualties, the injured were sent to the rear and housed in the three buildings that comprised Pennsylvania College. Two of those buildings—The President's House and Pennsylvania Hall—still stand and the site of the other—Linnean Hall—is marked.

"President's House" Gettysburg College

When Confederates drove the Union troops from their positions, they fled back across the campus being chased and shot at by the Southerners. Again emotions were at a fevered pitch: Northerners in fear of being shot or bayoneted in the back or captured to be sent to one of the horrid prisons, and Southerners, high with the sense that victory in battle—and perhaps this war—was right around the corner.

When the campus became the rear of the Confederate lines, their wounded were carried to the buildings being used by Union soldiers. Once wounded, the men sought to harm one another no more, and lay peacefully, side-by-side, awaiting recovery, the horror of the surgeon's saw, or death.

Pennsylvania Hall was one of the largest buildings in the area, and, thanks to preservation efforts by Gettysburg College, looks on the outside virtually as it did during the battle. The inside has been renovated to contain the Administration offices. Its modernized interior is what lends an incredulity to one of the most famous ghost stories of Gettysburg. For it was in this modern setting within this ancient edifice that two present day administrators were plunged into the horror of a Civil War Hospital[2]

WARNING: Gettysburg College has its own security police force. You do not have permission to enter any of the buildings for an investigation.

How to Get There

Pennsylvania Hall is accessible from the Washington Street entrance (at the west end of Stevens Street) to Gettysburg College. Park on Stevens Street or Washington Street (the parking on this part of the campus is restricted to Administrators and Students) and walk through the gates facing Washington Street. The large white columned structure before you is Pennsylvania Hall.

Linnean Hall stood on the site where the stone monolithic sculpture "The Sentinel" now stands to the west of Pennsylvania Hall. Careful examination of the ground may even reveal one of the cornerstones of the building.

"The President's House," as it has been called ever since Professor Henry L. Baugher became president of Pennsylvania College in 1852, is the large, white, two-story structure to the southwest of Pennsylvania Hall. In 2004, it was renamed the Norris-Wachob Alumni House.

Tips on Investigating

While the college campus is open to visitors, and Pennsylvania Hall is accessible by students, faculty, and administrators, the building is not open to the general public.

Any investigation must be done outside the buildings. The grounds were filled with wounded, temporary graves, and piles of amputated limbs, so an investigation should prove fruitful, especially outside of Pennsylvania Hall, "The President's House," or the site of Linnean Hall.

The problem, of course, is that the campus is usually filled with students during the school year and often populated with groups during the summer. Occasionally, however, there are periods in the summer between groups when the campus grows quiet.

HAUNTED OUT-OF-THE-WAY PLACES

East Cavalry Battlefield

On July 3, 1863, while Pickett's Charge fought itself out just south of the town of Gettysburg, a huge cavalry battle was taking place about three miles east of Gettysburg at what has come to be known as "East Cavalry Battlefield."

Confederate cavalry commander Major General James Ewell Brown ("J.E.B.") Stuart was ordered by General Lee to swing in a wide arc around the Union Army's right flank. While on the mission, Stuart ran into Union cavalry posted on the crossroads of the Low Dutch and Hanover Roads. The fighting began in the morning of July 3, and climaxed with a massive Confederate cavalry charge at about 3:00 P.M.

Pennsylvania Cavalry Monument

Posted on the left flank of Stuart's charge was Union Captain William Miller and his command, the 3rd Pennsylvania Cavalry. Miller had been told to hold his position, but was astounded when he saw the entire left flank of

Stuart's charging column passing within striking distance of his mounted men. An opportunity like this could not be missed and he asked his Lieutenant, William Brooke-Rawle, if he would back him up should he disobey orders and charge the enemy. Brooke-Rawle agreed and Miller ordered his men to charge.

They sailed into the huge Confederate column about two-thirds of the way back and drove almost completely through it until their charge lost its impetus and the Confederates began a retreat. Instead of being court-martialed for disobeying an order, Miller was eventually presented with the Congressional Medal of Honor. . .thirty-four years later.

For years, a mysterious form was seen wandering through the National Cemetery at Gettysburg at dusk, or sometimes late at night, long after the cemetery is closed to the public. A few people, including park rangers, got a fairly good look at him and described him as wearing a broad hat, dark blue uniform and high cavalry boots. Some say that it was Miller who had been seen floating through the cemetery, a mere wraith, disgruntled at not only the three-and-a-half decades it took to receive his medal, but that it was not even noted on his headstone. Whoever the ghost in the cavalry uniform was that wandered the National Cemetery, he has not been seen since Captain William Miller's tombstone was corrected in the early 1970's. . .

Warning: East Cavalry Battlefield Roads close at the posted closing time. Please conclude any investigation by then.

How to Get There

The easiest way to find East Cavalry Battlefield is to start from Lincoln Square in Gettysburg. Take Route 30/116 (York Street) East. When the road splits, bear right and continue to follow Route 116 East. After about two and one-half miles, begin to look for the National Park Service signs to East Cavalry Battlefield and take their marked tour.

Begin on the Union-held side of the field. Follow the signs for the tour until you reach the monument for the 3rd Pennsylvania Cavalry, a shaft off the road about 50 yards to the right. This is the point from which Captain Miller launched his attack into the Confederate Cavalry's left flank, helping to break the back of their assault.

Tips on Investigating

East Cavalry Field, although somewhat out of the way, is an excellent place for an investigation: quiet, secluded, rich in history, waiting to be explored. There are three areas on East Cavalry Battlefield that have yielded good results: The monument to the 3rd Pennsylvania Cavalry; the Michigan Cavalry Shaft; and the Confederate side of the field.

On December 2, 1999, a fellow investigator and I conducted an investigation at the monument to the 3rd Pennsylvania Cavalry, where I knew Captain Miller had launched the daring and deadly attack on the flank of Stuart's charging column of cavalry. Precisely where we stood, horsemen aligned themselves, screwed up their courage for the coming assault, ducked unconsciously when shells burst overhead, and tried to keep their horses from dashing away in panic. I tried to talk with the long-departed Medal of Honor recipient, Captain Miller, and some of his subordinates, like William Brooke-Rawle and other brave men of the 3rd. Using my digital recorder, I was successful in picking up some short answers to my questions, some garbled mumblings, and one loud response after addressing Lieutenant Brooke-Rawle. My fellow investigator was having wonderful success in photographing orbs, which seemed to be gathering around me as I recorded E.V.P.

Were they curious as to what I was doing with the strange contraption that spoke back in their voices? Perhaps. Or were they intent upon answering my questions—approaching the recorder in my hand, as if the only way they could communicate with it electromagnetically was to touch it? Or were they gathering together again as of old, to attack the enemy and secure the Union of States?

In one of the photos taken that night, are several orbs lined up. The line of orbs appeared to be at about the same height as men on horseback.

Prior to starting the investigation I had set up a camcorder to record our session. As we turned to walk back to the van, we apparently were not alone. When I reviewed the tape, numerous orbs were seen, "escaping" from us, flying away from our approach and directly at the camcorder, then dodging away at the last second to avoid the machine.

Later, after everything was packed up, my fellow investigator suddenly shouted, "There goes an orb!" I saw nothing, but she had seen an orb come *through* the windshield and pass leisurely between us. She snapped a picture. The photo showed the reflection of the flash in the rear window, but just to the left of that was a distinct orb.

That one of us saw the orb and the other did not is an example of how some people are more sensitive than others when it comes to the paranormal.

How to Get to the Michigan Cavalry Shaft

Continue along the road about a quarter of a mile to the Michigan Cavalry Shaft on the left hand side.

Tips on Investigating

At the Michigan Cavalry Shaft I singled out the Michigan troops' most famous commander, George Armstrong Custer. I reasoned that the troopers from Michigan would certainly have known the name Custer, whether they had died at Gettysburg or had lived beyond Custer's 1876 fated rendezvous with Sitting Bull at the Little Big Horn.

In my initial attempt at gathering E.V.P., I got unintelligible, one syllable answers to the questions "Are you Union cavalrymen?" and "Are you from Michigan?" In total silence, I watched the LED numbers on my Panasonic recorder begin to move. The numbers continued to roll by after the next two questions. When I played the recording back, this was what I got:

M.N.: "Are you following General Custer?"
Male voice: "Yes, Sir."
M.N.: "Do you like General Custer?"
Male voice: "Yes, Sir."
M.N.: "Does General Custer come here?"
Male voice: "Yes."

The second set of questions I asked at the Michigan Cavalry Shaft yielded some garbled answers, and one startlingly clear announcement.

M.N.: "Were you buried here?"
Male voice: "In town."

Directions to the Confederate Side of the Battlefield

Drive until the road dead-ends at the small parking area. You will pass Confederate cannons lined up along the road.

At the side of the battlefield held by the Confederates my effort to get a good E.V.P. session was being upset by the noise of geese flying over head. Frustrated, standing in the darkened woods of the Confederate battle lines, I burst out with, "Did you ever hear of Robert E. Lee?" The absurdity of my question to Confederate soldiers hit me and, instead of pausing the full 40 seconds in silence, I blurted out, "Silly question, huh?"

Someone else thought it was a pretty stupid question, for recorded between the question and my own answer, was a loud, raspy, seemingly angry "Yes!"

Directions Back to Gettysburg

Although you may follow the road that leads through the woods to the left, it's better to retrace your drive to Low Dutch Road, then out to Route 116 and back to Gettysburg.

SACHS COVERED BRIDGE

Sachs Covered Bridge was crossed by both Union and Confederate troops during the Battle of Gettysburg, and the surrounding land became a hospital and burial site for the Confederates. It has long been a fine fishing hole, a biker's destination, and secluded romantic area for generations of Adams Countians. The bridge was built in 1852, and for a decade its most sinister role was helping farmers get their goods from one side of Marsh Creek to the other. Then, after the first few days of July 1863, its role forever changed.

Sachs Covered Bridge

On July 1, Doubleday's Division of the Union Army's First Corps crossed the bridge to get to the battle. More Union infantry and artillery crossed it later, into the evening of July 1.

On July 2, the Confederates began to arrive and took over the area around the bridge. The bridge and the surrounding land, and the cooling waters of Marsh Creek below it, became the scene of succor for Confederates wounded in the vicious fighting just a couple miles to the east. Many died and were buried nearby. It would be seven or more years before anyone would get to their forlorn, abandoned graves to remove their remains to their homes in the South. Many would never leave. Today, where fishermen try to land the evening's meal, or would-be suitors try their best lines on their female companions, forgotten souls stir on the bridge and in the woods to disrupt many a well-planned evening.

WARNING: Because of the large number of individuals visiting the bridge after dark, the area has been closed and is patrolled after dark. Dusk might be a good time to visit for photos or video. Since it is a quiet place, anytime during the day would be good to attempt E.V.P.

How to Get There

Follow Route 15 South out of Gettysburg. At the first crossroads (The Peach Orchard and Wheatfield Road), turn right. Follow that road past the first stop sign at West Confederate Avenue, down the hill past the Eisenhower Farm, and to the second modern bridge. Slow down as you are approaching this second bridge. Turn left immediately after the bridge and follow the road to the end.

Tips on Investigating

Water seems to be one of the elements that attracts and fosters spirit activity. Sachs Bridge, and the area around it, seem to release their ghosts according to their own whim. The most successful investigations have invested a great deal of time at the bridge, videotaping, photographing, and attempting to record E.V.P. Though occasionally, a one-time visit will result in a paranormal experience.

Investigators have seen individuals at the end of the bridge farthest from the parking area. A man and his family saw what they described as a man in a Civil War era "slouch" hat slumped over in an old-fashioned wheelchair. . .at a time when there was no wheelchair access and no cars—other than theirs—parked at the bridge.

One night, as paranormal investigators set up their video camera at the parking-lot end of the bridge, a group of college students came running, terrified, screaming about the sound of horses chasing them. Replaying the video camera showed orbs racing towards it, following them.

Events are not confined to the bridge. People have seen what appears to be a man carrying a lantern walking down the dirt road that runs along the bank of Marsh Creek; he stops, he beckons, but to where, no one knows.

The far end of the bridge was, on one pre-dawn Halloween morning, for me a place of strange happenings. Karyol Kirkpatrick, famed psychic, was at that end of the bridge. When asked if she wanted to go into the woods beyond, she exclaimed an emphatic "No!", something I had never heard her do. In fact, she wanted to return to the vehicle. After being questioned further, she said she just did not have the energy to deal with the evil that was in those woods.

A few minutes later, I was with another investigator at that end of the bridge. She held my night-vision scope; I had my digital camera. On a feeling, a whim, I raised the camera and snapped a picture into the darkness of the roof of the bridge. At the same time, the other investigator shouted, "Oh, I just saw something go by!" I brought up the photo on my camera, and there it was: a classic shot of paranormal mist in the shape of a "ghost" with "arms" outstretched; alongside it was an orb. The other investigator exclaimed, "That was just what I saw!"[1]

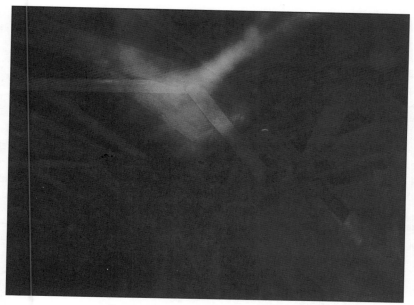

Paranormal Mist at Sachs Bridge

HERR TAVERN AND PUBLICK HOUSE
WARNING! Herr Tavern and Publick House is a privately owned Bed & Breakfast and fine restaurant and is not open for a general investigation. Overnight guests and diners, however, are graciously welcomed.

Frederick Herr's Tavern was around long before the Battle of Gettysburg began in his front yard. On the morning of July 1, 1863, Confederate troops advanced past the house and buildings of the early 19th Century landmark. Confederate artillery lined up at the top of Herr's Ridge where the Tavern sits. Soon the tavern and outbuildings became makeshift hospital and recovery sites. A shell crashed into one corner of the house. From the upper floors, much of the epic battle could be seen.

There have been a number of reports of overnight guests being touched, of unseen individuals pressing down upon the bedsheets in the middle of the night, doorknobs being rattled in the pre-dawn hours, phones being tampered with, and workers being pushed while on ladders.

How to Get There

From Gettysburg's Lincoln Square, follow Route 30 West. Herr's Tavern will be on the left at the corner of Route 30 and Herr Ridge Road.

Tips on Investigating

The downstairs is kept active (by the living!) with one of Gettysburg's finer restaurants. If you really want to do an investigation, stay overnight in one of the beautiful rooms they offer.

The former owners, Frederick and Susan Herr, seem to be still very active in the administration of the Tavern and Publick House, checking on invisible children who cry, singing light opera, and doing a door check at 3:00 A.M.. . .well over a century after their deaths. Louie the Robber appears occasionally to visit the cellar of the Tavern House, scene of his counterfeiting escapades in the 19th Century.

You may also want to refer to some of the individual room "diaries." They are peppered with comments from overnight guests referring to odd, paranormal goings on.[2]

Hospital Sites on the Outskirts of Town

If high levels of human emotion leave their imprint upon their surroundings as "residual hauntings," then there cannot be any more haunted sites than the places where temporary hospitals were set up to administer to the tens of thousands of wounded that were the tragic result of the three days of fighting at Gettysburg.

Although they are removed from the well-known Park boundaries, many areas that were once hospital sites have been purchased and preserved by the National Park Service at Gettysburg. You will find several "Hospital Woods" in their historic files and numerous references to various farms outside the Park's boundaries. Many of the hospital sites are marked by blue and gray metal signs at the entrance to the properties.

WARNING! Nearly all of the hospital sites off the National Park are privately owned. A sign in front of a house signifying it was a hospital does not give you permission to trespass. Reading this book or carrying

it with you does not give you permission to trespass on private farms! Respect homeowner's rights in any investigation!

Some hospital sites, however, are publicly owned and are either accessible to enter, or to approach to get near enough for an investigation.

CAMP LETTERMAN

After the battle, authorities realized that the patients in the scattered field hospitals should be gathered together to be treated and, with any luck, sent home. On July 20, 1863, Camp Letterman was established about a mile east of Gettysburg on the York Road. The camp had easy access to a railroad for the evacuation of those patients recovered enough to travel, plenty of shade, and a spring of fresh water. The area had been known to Gettysburgians since before the battle as a picnic site with plenty of cool, fresh air.

Two weeks after the battle Camp Letterman held about 1600 wounded. Rows of tents housed both Union and Confederate wounded, still too sick to travel to either a main hospital in the North (for the Union soldiers) or a prison camp (for the unfortunate Confederates). In addition to the hospital tents, there were tents for officers, nurses, surgeons, and the United States Sanitary Commission. Ominously, there, in the tent row farthest from the road, was the "Dead House," where those were taken who, after surviving their horrific wounds in battle, succumbed to infection. In the same row were the embalming tent and the camp graveyard.

How to Get There

From Lincoln Square follow Route 30 East about a mile. On the right hand side you will see a large stone Government marker indicating the site of Camp Letterman.

Tips on Investigating

The site of Camp Letterman is privately owned, but some areas of the parking lot in the developed area (currently a Giant Food market), are located on the site. Photos can be taken from the Government marker or parts of the parking lot, but may be contaminated by modern lights. E.V.P. attempts may also fail since the site is so close to a major highway.

HOSPITAL WOODS

No sooner did the fighting begin on the morning of July 1, 1863, when wounded men began to make their way painfully back behind the lines. As soon as army surgeons began to establish "aide stations," usually in shady woods, preferably near a stream or spring, the torn bodies began to trickle into them. One such station which quickly grew into a field hospital was in the woods along Willoughby Run, just to the south of the Chambersburg Pike. Some of those woods still exist along Country Club Lane and are owned by the National Park Service.

How to Get There

From Lincoln Square follow Route 30 West. Pass over McPherson's Ridge and descend into the valley of Willoughby Run. Once over the modern highway bridge you will see the Gettysburg Country Club on the left. Just past the entrance to the Country Club is Country Club Lane. Turn left and follow Country Club Lane as it curves left. Continue to follow the Lane and the woods will be on your right the entire length of Country Club Lane to the stop sign.

Tips on Investigating

The woods are owned by the National Park Service but are not marked as closed after Park hours. It is not recommended, however, that you investigate after dark. The possibility of falling and injuring yourself in the dark is real. Choose a time around dusk to investigate, or possibly around dawn. The woods are in a residential area, so respect the privacy of the homeowners in the area. Do not park on their property or in their driveways.

HOSPITAL ROAD

Hospital Road runs from the Baltimore Pike towards the Taneytown Road. One of the first hospital markers you will come to is the marker for the Second Corps Hospital. It was in the Spangler Farm just beyond this marker where Confederate Brigadier General Lewis A. Armistead died. Armistead was the officer who led the 300-or-so Confederates over the wall during the climax of Pickett's Charge and fell, mortally wounded, in the effort. Testimony by occupants of the farmhouse recall the story of the previous family being awakened by the clanking of buckets. Looking out the window, they see a man dressed in a long white duster—like those used by hospital orderlies—carrying empty buckets to where the old well—now dried up and gone—once was. He acts like he is filling the buckets, then, burdened, returns to the house and enters. Rushing downstairs to confront the stranger, the family finds. . .no one.

Warning! While Hospital Road is open all night long, the homes and farms along it are privately owned. Be respectful of their privacy. Do not drive into private drives.

Hospital Road

How to Get There

Follow the Baltimore Road south from Gettysburg. Go over Cemetery Hill, travel about a mile, turn right on Granite School House Lane. Follow Granite School House Lane to the sign for Hospital Road and bear left.

Tips on Investigating

As you follow the road you will pass a number of the large government markers denoting field hospitals of the various Union Army Corps and Divisions. This area may yield some results, especially with E.V.P., since it is a little out of the way and, in some spots, far enough from a major road to be quiet.

Photography may work well here too, since it is not closed to the public and can be visited well into the night.

In attempts at E.V.P., you might try using the names of Armistead or the various Corps to summon the men as you stop along Hospital Road at the various markers.

CONCLUSION

It is fascinating to ponder what reverberations there would be if, suddenly, one of us discovers that, without a doubt, the Dead live and that we can communicate with them. How would that change the world? What vast knowledge would we gain from the Dead that might help—or harm—our current passage through life? What would that discovery do to the human emotion of grief? Of the fear of death? Of the crime of murder and dread of capital punishment? Of the principles of suicide and martyrdom? Would the knowledge that Death had lost its eternal sting make this a better world or worse?

As with all knowledge, the answer lies, if it ever comes, in how we use it.

Although the main subject of this book is paranormal investigations at Gettysburg, that is not to say that these techniques and protocols will work *only* in Gettysburg. The procedures explained are good, solid principles that will work investigating any allegedly haunted site, whether battlefields, burial sites, or buildings.

If you find yourself becoming more interested in the paranormal, you may want to keep a scrapbook of newspaper clippings, articles, and quotes from various books on the subject. If you live or work in what seems to be a haunted house, apartment, building or site, it is imperative that you keep a journal of seemingly unexplainable events, complete with dates, times, weather conditions, names of witnesses, and other information that could lead to discovering patterns about the events. If they cannot be explained away by simple observations of actual happenings, enough anecdotal evidence will supply data from which patterns can be extrapolated.

I maintain a non-solicitation policy concerning the stories I collect and publish in my *Ghosts of Gettysburg* books. However, if you have done a serious investigation, utilized the techniques taught in this book, completed the *Ghost Investigation Checklist*, and obtained documented results, I would be interested in receiving a copy of the report. Your report will be archived and preserved for posterity. It will, no doubt, be used eventually in a survey of paranormal happenings and will contribute to the body of data about Gettysburg. . .and beyond.

APPENDIX A: A THEORETICAL APPROACH
TO THE PARANORMAL

In 1991, Michael Talbot published a book entitled *The Holographic Universe*. Talbot takes the work of David Bohn, Ph.D., Karl Pribram, Ph. D., and other far-sighted physicists to further a model of the universe, and reality as we know it, as a giant hologram: ". . .there is evidence to suggest that our world and everything in it–from snowflakes to maple trees to falling stars and spinning electrons–are also only ghostly images, projections from a level of reality so beyond our own it is literally beyond space and time."

Talbot went on to write that our human brains act as "filters" for a world composed only of a "frequency domain" of resonating wave forms. From solid rock mountains to electrons and other subatomic particles (which cannot be measured because they have no dimension and can be both particle and wave), he explains that there is a deeper, enfolded, more primary level of reality which underlies and gives birth to our own level of existence.

Talbot uses this new paradigm of our universe—our "reality" as a hologram with an underlying reality—to explain not only the actions of mountains and sub-atomic particles, but brings it to a personal level: how dreaming can be a bridge to this sub-strata of reality where we actually visit a parallel universe; how "miracles" like stigmata, or mass healings, or mass visions, or psychokinesis are produced by tapping into that level of reality. Materializations and dematerializations of physical objects, too, ("apports" in paranormal lingo) are manifestations of another world co-existing with the one in which we "live." It may also be the place where "spirits" go to dwell until they choose—or are allowed by special circumstances—to reincarnate into the visible, everyday reality.

These special circumstances can be related to a place—such as Gettysburg with all its granite and quartz—or to past events—once again like Gettysburg (or Antietam or Normandy Beach or Iwo Jima) that produced an overwhelming amount of human energy through personal tragedy or extinction. They can be related to natural events—such as the time of year, like the change in seasons, or the change from day to night, or—believe it or not—the waning and waxing moon, or sun flares. The circumstances by which spirits may incarnate may also be related to random accidents in the wave structures or frequencies of the energy around us.

The age-old phenomena of "auras," or human energy fields, to Talbot is evidence of Pribram's theory of a "frequency domain" beyond normal perceptive abilities which only certain trained or uniquely gifted individuals can see. He references UCLA's Professor Valerie Hunt who proposes that the human energy field is more than just electromagnetic: "We have a feeling that it is much more complex and without a doubt composed of an as yet undiscovered energy. . ." which apparently has a higher frequency or vibration than regular matter/energy. She and others have determined, with independent scientific experimentation, that the very human aspects that reflect "mind," such as creativity, spirituality, and imagination are based in this energy field. Such studies may scientifically and experimentally prove that the flesh and blood brain and the "Mind" are indeed two separate entities—with the brain located in the head, and the "Mind" located in the human energy field and, as such, a part of the vast, resonating, underlying reality which can be tapped into by the brain. In this field, "Mind" may also retain its individual personality, just as an individual wave retains certain particular characteristics, such as speed and height, even while moving through the ocean.

This frequency domain—the vast, universal, energy field of which the personal human energy field is a part—is indestructible and eternal. Resonating at a different rate than that which we are used to, it is also undetectable to most of us. As a resonating energy field, it is possible for us to tune in to that frequency domain, like a radio tunes in to radio waves. Being able to tune in to that specific frequency—whether accidentally or purposefully—means we have an opportunity for a vision into the domain where the personal "Mind" dwells. A "ghost," or paranormal events such as unexplainable noises, smells, touchings, or feelings, may be the manifestation of this vision or intrusion into that other world.[1]

This frequency domain, or energy field, begins to sound very much like the afterlife dwelling-place.

The holographic model of reality and its substrata may account for the three-dimensionality of ghosts, since waves carry all kinds of three-dimensional information within them, such as height, breadth, duration, and so forth. But waves need a medium—like water or air—through which to travel and carry their information.

Mainstream physicists, such as Einstein and Max Planck, came to realize that space—rather than being a vacuum—was full of activity with particles exchanging energy and constantly coming into and going out of existence. The energy thus is constant and inexhaustible. It is also everywhere. It is called the Zero Point Field.

A "field"—like an electromagnetic field or gravitational field—literally has no boundaries. It connects one part of the universe to all other parts. This suggests that everything is interconnected by waves, just like electromagnetic waves spread out invisibly and touch everything, to the farthest reaches of the universe. Scientists speculate that the Zero Point Field also touches the past and the future, which may provide a link to the paranormal.

The famous philosopher's cause and effect question asks: If a butterfly waves its wings in Asia, does that—in causing air molecules to bump into one another in a chain reaction—have an effect on events in North America? Apparently, with the Zero Point Field this is true, but on a scale that transcends distance, space, and time, both past and future. Could this be the link between people, events, scenes, feelings, and smells, that have happened before our existence and our observations of them now, as apparitions, in the present?

The fascinating thing about waves is that while they carry encoded information about the energy within them, when they collide they accumulate information about each other. They have an infinite capacity for information storage and, therefore, can carry and transmit virtually everything that has happened while the wave was in existence, as well as pass the information on infinitely.[2]

On a related note, biologist Rupert Sheldrake has proposed what he has named the "morphogenetic" field, similar to the electromagnetic field that invisibly surrounds us, yet carrying not energy, but information. A morphogenetic field, for Sheldrake, explains how information is shared across time and space. This information field would explain everything from how crystals grow in the same molecular patterns over the eons, to the sharing of the subconscious collectively, to why flocks of birds and schools of fish all turn at precisely the same time without communication.

According to Sheldrake, the brain is not so much a repository of information as it is a receiver. Instead of recalling information from within, it tunes in to the appropriate information which resides in the vast "field" surrounding us. The field is a collective memory throughout all nature expressed through morphic resonance. That suggests there is no real separation between minds—both those present and past, including those living and dead.

If the morphogenetic field exists as Sheldrake explains it, consciousness, thoughts, and mental processes all exist in the field through time and remain without the physical brain to support them. According to Robert Gilman, an associate of Sheldrake, "This would allow the existence of non-physical beings." The key to accessing this field is attuning to its resonance.

Terence McKenna, another of Sheldrake's colleagues, queried, "Do you think this morphic resonance could be regarded as a possible explanation for the phenomena of spirits and other metaphysical entities, and can the method of evoking beings from the spirit world be simply a case of cracking the morphic code?"[3]

I have my own theories. In the ocean, waves travel from different points, albeit in a limited "field," with the limit being the surface or the shore. Occasionally, randomly, waves will come together with the same resonance, combine, and form what is known as a "rogue" wave. In a body of water, this convergence sets up exactly the right conditions for strange events to occur and for the medium—water—to act differently than it normally does. Tidal waves form; huge "rogue" waves emerge and swamp ships; giant "bubbles"or "troughs" appear, decreasing the buoyancy of the water, and ships sink. Perhaps similarly, if energy is stored within the rocks or earth of the geology of Gettysburg, or in the fieldstone, brick, and wood walls that once sheltered the dying sons of heartbroken mothers, is it possible, under the right atmospheric conditions or perhaps the right emotional condition of the observer, for the electromagnetic or morphogenetic waves to "sync," and resonate so as to become accessible again to human senses? There is, in the study of sound, the phenomenon of a "standing wave," when sound waves in a room converge on one spot to produce a "pool" of energy that is harmonic in nature. Could this be what happens to other types of wave energy–paranormal electromagnetic waves or Pribram's "frequency domain" waves—when they focus in harmonic resonance and form ghostly images or sounds?

In the vast, multi-dimensional wave frequency proposed by modern theoretical physicists—the Zero Point Field—or within Sheldrake's morphogenetic information field, could "rogue" waves be generated by the combining of smaller waves, and in their combining and resonance produce paranormal phenomena?

Everything from a fleeting glimpse into the past, complete with individuals dressed for the period, to physical objects being moved, to sounds and voices, to being physically touched or feeling a chill, to mere "feelings" such as intuition, may be the manifestation of these ubiquitous waves coming together, peaking and ebbing energy, or information, at just the right time to be observed and experienced by humans. In other words, the dead and all their worlds are here with us, right next to us at all times, just at a frequency we are not tuned to. We have to wait until the right combinations of wave frequency—when *it* randomly tunes itself to *us*—to experience the paranormal.

But that also opens up the possibility of *us* tuning into *it*. Everyone is aware that the brain also gives off electrical information via waves. We can observe how the brain is functioning by using the electroencephalograph which reads the brain's waves. Eastern yogis are adept at training their brains, through breathing and concentration techniques, to accomplish many seemingly impossible things. These are accomplished, they admit, by altering the frequency of the energy in their brains by tuning into an energy greater than themselves, a universal power that is all around, all powerful, and eternal.

Many ghost investigators can intuitively turn, snap a picture, and get paranormal results. This, they claim is from experience, or from just allowing their mind to tell them when to react. By using techniques of mind-training, or even using the ghost-detecting instruments for bio-feedback, can humans eventually tune in to the resonance that apparently is all around us?

With the proper training and practice, can any of us—or all of us—someday tune in to the wisdom of the ages?

APPENDIX B: ADDITIONAL RESEARCH FOR PICKETT'S CHARGE

Addressing the individuals or units by name can facilitate communicating with them through E.V.P. or drawing them near for photographs.

Other Brigades that were in Pickett's Division, besides Armistead's, were Garnett's Brigade and Kemper's Brigade.

Regiments for Garnett's Brigade: 8th Virginia (from Loudon County); 18th Virginia (Pittsylvania County); 19th Virginia (Albemarle County); 28th Virginia (Roanoke County) and the 56th Virginia. Brigade commander Richard Brooke Garnett was born in Essex County, Virginia. Unlike most of the rest of the Confederate officers in the Charge, Garnett, being ill on July 3, rode his horse into the fray. He was shot down and his body never identified or recovered.

James Lawson Kemper commanded the third brigade in Pickett's Division and also rode into the fight. He would be seriously wounded. Kemper's Brigade consisted of the 1st Virginia, commanded by Colonel Lewis B. Williams, and was recruited mostly in and around Richmond. It included the famous company "The Richmond Greys." Williams died during the Charge in a bizarre way. A shell burst near his horse. As Williams fell to the ground, he landed upon his own sword, committing inadvertent suicide. He is buried in Richmond's Hollywood Cemetery.

The 3rd Virginia Regiment was commanded by Colonel Joseph Mayo, Jr. Many of the 3rd Virginia Regiment's companies had names which might be helpful in connecting with them: Company A - "The Dismal Swamp Rangers" from Portsmouth; Company B - "The Virginia Rifles"; Company C - "The Dinwiddie Greys" from Dinwiddie County; Company D - "The Southampton Greys" from Southampton County; Company E - "The Cockade Rifles" from Petersburg; Company G - "The Rough and Ready Guards" from Southampton County; Company H - "The National Greys" from Portsmouth; Company K - "The Halifax Rifles" from Halifax County.

The 7th Virginia Regiment was commanded by Colonel W. Tazewell Patton, great-uncle of World War II General George Patton. The modern General Patton was well known for his belief in the supernatural, and it apparently was passed down through the family to him. "Taz" Patton had, in the past, several premonitions of being struck by bullets in battle, as he did just before the Battle of Gettysburg. This time he was fatally right: he was mortally wounded during the Charge. In addition to the prescient Tazewell Patton, other names that might be helpful in connecting with those who fought and died on this very ground are the company nicknames: Company A - "The Richardson Guards" of Madison County; Company B - "The Washington Greys" of Rappahannock County; Company C - "Captain John C. Porter's Company" of Culpeper County; Company D - "The Giles Volunteers" of Giles County; Company E - "The Hazewood Volunteers" of Culpeper County; Company F - "Captain F. M. McMillan's Company"; Company G -"Rappahannock Guard" of Rappahannock County; Company I - "The Holcombe Guards" of Albemarle County; Company K - "The Madison Greys" of Madison County; and "The Brandy Rifles" from Culpeper.

Other distinctive names from the 11th Virginia Regiment are "The Lynchburg Rifle Greys," "The Southern Guards," "The Clifton Greys," "The Fincastle Rifles," "The Lynchburg Rifles," "The Preston Guards," "The Lynchburg Home Guard," "The Jeff Davis Guard," "The Rough and Ready Rifles," and "The Valley Regulators."

Finally, the 24th Virginia's companies names: "The Floyd Riflemen," "The Carroll Boys," "The New River Rifles," and "The Henry Guards."

ENDNOTES

What is a Ghost?

1. Hill and Williams, *The Supernatural,* p. 95.
2. See Nesbitt, *Ghosts of Gettysburg VI,* pp. 44-45 for two stories of a woman projecting her spiritual body to sites other than where her physical body was.
3. See Nesbitt, *Ghosts of Gettysburg,* "An Authentic Reenactment," p. 50.
4. See Nesbitt, *Ghosts of Gettysburg,* "The Tireless Surgeons of Old Dorm," pp. 54-58.
5. See Nesbitt, *More Ghosts of Gettysburg,* "Slaying Days in Eden," pp.17-26, "Off-Off Broadway," pp. 54-55, and "Fall of the Sparrow," pp. 68-71.
6. Warren, Joshua P. *How to Hunt Ghosts: A Practical Guide.* Warren does a fine job of organizing the plethora of data concerning ghosts.
7. See Nesbitt, *Ghosts of Gettysburg VI,* "The Substance of Shadows," for an excellent account of a NDE (Near Death Experience).
8. Bartholomew, "Afterlife: The Scientific Case for the Human Soul," *Reader's Digest,* August, 2003, pp. 123-128.
9. McTaggart, Lynne *The Field: The Quest for the Secret Force of the Universe.*
10. Sheldrake, Rubert, *Dogs that Know When Their Owners are Coming Home,* NY: Crown Publishers, 1999. pp. 274-277.
11. See Nesbitt, *More Ghosts of Gettysburg,* pp. 21-22.
12. Author Katherine Ramsland, during an investigation at Herr Tavern asked the entities present to show themselves, whereupon, one moved in front of her video camera lens, moved quickly around in a strange "dance," then, as if suddenly becoming self-conscious, zoomed away like a shy child.

Why Ghosts Exist at Gettysburg

1. Those interested in investigating battle sites of the Gettysburg Campaign are encouraged to refer to some of the books mentioned in the "Resources" section of this book. Some are quite near Gettysburg like Hunterstown, Carlisle, and Hanover; the farthest, like Culpeper, Virginia, are only a couple of hours away. My own book *35 Days to Gettysburg* chronicles, day by day, the routes along which parts of both armies marched, reconstructed on modern highways.

Gettysburg: The Paranormal Experience

[1] The photo was taken by Carlyle and Becky Rell and is on display at the *Ghosts of Gettysburg Candlelight Walking Tour* Headquarters.

[2] Morse, Melvin, M.D., "The Right Temporal Lobe and Associated Limbic Lobe Structures as the Biological Interface with an Interconnected Universe." www.astralpulse.com/articles/others/articles_34.htm.

[3] Coco, Greg, *A Strange and Blighted Land*, p.34.

[4] See Nesbitt, *Ghosts of Gettysburg IV*, pp. 39-42.

[5] Morse, Melvin, M.D. *Transformed by the Light*, as quoted in www.direct.ca/trinity/shroud1.html.

[6] I-mass.com/turn0402.html

How to Investigate the Paranormal

[1] The entire recording of this "conversation" is available on the CD *GhostHunts*, by Jim Cooke and Mark Nesbitt, a collection of paranormal investigations done in the last several years. It is available through the internet at www.ghostsofgettysburg.com, or in the *Ghosts of Gettysburg Candlelight Walking Tours* Headquarters at 271 Baltimore Street, Gettysburg, PA.

[2] Julie Pellegrino, a local "sensitive," recommended that I pause for four or five breaths before asking the next question; she said she "heard" (psychically, of course) the spirits did not have enough time to respond when I only paused twenty seconds between questions. She was right. I have had more success with longer pauses between questions.

Where to look for Ghosts in Gettysburg

[1] It has often been said that "Gettysburg was the largest battle ever on the North American continent," but we don't know that for sure. There have always been the persistent rumors since the 19th Century of a great Native American struggle about a mile west of what is now known as Big Round Top, involving, it has been said, more combatants than were engaged in the 1863 battle, and killing and wounding even more. That is another reason why the area in and around Gettysburg could be haunted with the spirits of dead warriors.

[2] As witnessed by Sgt. Charles Blanchard, quoted in Gregory Coco's *A Strange and Blighted Land,* p. 89.

[3] Ibid., pp. 89-90.

[4] Ibid, p. 141.

[5] A letter in my personal archives mentions the re-burial of the remains of a soldier found some years after the battle in the back yard of a house on

Baltimore Street. To the best of my knowledge, this fact has never been revealed before and so we must assume the bones of this unknown soldier still rest in the unmarked grave in someone's back yard.

⁶ I was approached once by a man who invited me out to his Civil War era barn on Hospital Road. He said that virtually every time he took a picture inside the structure, which once held the torn bodies of the battle's castoffs, it would be filled with orbs and misty ectoplasm.

Haunted Sites on the East Side of the Battlefield

¹ See Nesbitt, *Ghosts of Gettysburg VI,* pp. 78-88 for an explanation of "Shadow People."

² Coco, 19.

³ A detailed history and more ghost stories of Culp's Hill are found in Nesbitt's *Ghosts of Gettysburg,* pp.13-16 and *Ghosts of Gettysburg V,* pp.40-47.

⁴ Pfanz, Harry, *Gettysburg: Culp's Hill and Cemetery Hill*, pp.320-321.

⁵ Pfanz, Harry, *Gettysburg: Culp's Hill and Cemetery Hill,* pp. *235-259.*

Haunted Sites North of Gettysburg

¹ See Nesbitt, *Ghosts of Gettysburg V*, "Mysteries of Oak Ridge," for the full story of these encounters.

² Martin, David G. *Gettysburg: July 1*, pp. 271-291.

Haunted Sites on the West Side of the Battlefield

¹ See Nesbitt, *Ghosts of Gettysburg IV*, pp. 27-30.

² See Nesbitt, *Ghosts of Gettysburg III,* pp. 26-27.

³ See Nesbitt, *Ghosts of Gettysburg,* pp. 51-53.

⁴ Some other units in Pickett's Division were Garnett's Brigade and Kemper's Brigade. (See Appendix B for additional names and unit numbers that will help in connecting with them via E.V.P.

⁵ See Nesbitt, *Ghosts of Gettysburg V*, pp. 54-55.

⁶ See Nesbitt, *Ghosts of Gettysburg IV*, pp. 81-86.

⁷ See Nesbitt, *More Ghosts of Gettysburg,* pp. 27-33.

Haunted Sites on the South End of the Battlefield

¹ See Nesbitt, *Ghosts of Gettysburg,* pp. 17-20.

² See Nesbitt, *Ghosts of Gettysburg V*, p. 29.

³ See Nesbitt, *Ghosts of Gettysburg IV*, pp. 18-20.

⁴ See Nesbitt, *Ghosts of Gettysburg,* pp. 20-22 and *Ghosts of Gettysburg IV,* pp. 42-43.

⁵ Pfanz, *Gettysburg: The Second Day*, p.195.

⁶ Ibid, p. 231.

[7] "New York at Gettysburg," Vol. III, p. 953, reprinted in *The Gettysburg Papers*, compiled by Ken Bandy & Florence Freeland. Dayton: Morningside Bookshop, 1986.

[8] Coco, *A Strange and Blighted Land*, p. 30.

[9] Pfanz, *Gettysburg: The Second Day*, p. 257-260.

[10] The fighting in the Wheatfield was especially confused, with regiments being thrown in and withdrawn frequently. Perhaps the most concise book to help understand the action is *The Wheatfield at Gettysburg: A Walking Tour* by Jay Jorgensen (Gettysburg: Thomas Publications, 2002). *Gettysburg: The Second Day* by Harry W. Pfanz (Chapel Hill: The University of North Carolina Press, 1987) gives a more complete version.

Haunted Sites in The Town of Gettysburg

[1] A compete list of all the paranormal events which have occurred in "The Ghost House," is detailed in *Ghosts of Gettysburg VI*.

[2] For the complete story see Mark Nesbitt, *Ghosts of Gettysburg*, pp. 54-58.

Haunted Out-of-the-Way Places

[1] See Nesbitt, *Ghosts of Gettysburg IV*, "The Bridge to Nowhere," for some of the stories and background on Sachs Covered Bridge.

[2] See Nesbitt, *Ghosts of Gettysburg III*, "Arabesques Upon Water," for details and additional stories about Herr Tavern.

Appendix A: A Theoretical Approach to the Paranormal

[1] For further reading, see Michael Talbot's *The Holographic Universe*.

[2] For further reading, see Lynne McTaggart's *The Field*.

[3] "Morphogenetic Fields according to Robert Gilman, Terence McKenna and Rupert Sheldrake" at www.experiencefestival.com/a/Morphogenetic_fields.

RESOURCES

There are numerous books on Gettysburg and on Ghosts. Here are some of the printed materials to read to prepare for investigating Gettysburg.

Histories:

Coco, Gregory A. *A Strange and Blighted Land: Gettysburg: The Aftermath.* Gettysburg: Thomas Publications, 1995.

_____.*Wasted Valor: The Confederate Dead at Gettysburg.* Gettysburg: Thomas Publications, 1990.

_____. *A Vast Sea of Misery.* Gettysburg: Thomas Publications, 1988.

Frassanito, William A., *Gettysburg: A Journey in Time.* NY: Charles Scribner's Sons, 1975. Reprint. Gettysburg: Thomas Publications, 1996.

Jorgenson, Jay. *The Wheatfield at Gettysburg: A Walking Tour.* Gettysburg: Thomas Publications, 2002.

Martin, David G. *Gettysburg July 1.* PA: Combined Books, 1996.

Nesbitt, Mark V. *35 Days to Gettysburg: The Campaign Diaries of Two American Enemies.* Harrisburg: Stackpole Books, 1992.

Pfanz, Harry W. *Gettysburg: The Second Day.* Chapel Hill: The University of North Carolina Press, 1987.

Pfanz, Harry W. *Gettysburg: Culp's & Cemetery Hill.* Chapel Hill: The University of North Carolina Press, 1993.

Pfanz, Harry W. *Gettysburg: The First Day.* Chapel Hill: The University of North Carolina Press, 2001.

Rollins, Richard, ed. *Pickett's Charge! Eyewitness Accounts.* Redondo Beach, CA: Rank and File Publications, 1994.

Books Relating to Ghosts:

Guiley, Rosemary Ellen. *The Encyclopedia of Ghosts and Spirits,* Second Edition. NY: Checkmark Books, 2000.

Hill, Douglas and Pat Williams. *The Supernatural,* London: Bloomsbury Books, 1989.

Kaczmarek, Dale. *Field Guide to Spirit Photography.* Alton, IL: Whitechapel Productions Press, 2002.

Konstantinos. *Contact the Other Side: Seven Methods for Afterlife Communication.* St. Paul, MN: Llewellyn Publications, 2001.

Nesbitt, Mark. *Ghosts of Gettysburg.* Gettysburg: Thomas Publications, 1991.

_____. *More Ghosts of Gettysburg.* Gettysburg: Thomas Publications, 1992.

_____. *Ghosts of Gettysburg III.* Gettysburg: Thomas Publications, 1995.

_____. *Ghosts of Gettysburg IV.* Gettysburg: Thomas Publications, 1998.

_____. *Ghosts of Gettysburg V.* Gettysburg: Thomas Publications, 2000.

_____. *Ghosts of Gettysburg VI.* Gettysburg: Second Chance Publications, 2004.

Taylor, Troy. *The Ghost Hunter's Guidebook: The Essential Handbook for Ghost Research.* Alton, IL: Whitechapel Productions Press, 2001.

Warren, Joshua P. *How to Hunt Ghosts: A Practical Guide.* New York: Simon & Schuster, 2003.

Books on Related Subjects:

McTaggart, Lynne. *The Field: The Quest for the Secret Force of the Universe.* NY: Harper Collins Publishers, 2002.

Mitchell, Dr. Edgar. *The Way of the Explorer.* New York: G. P. Putnam's Sons, 1996.

Moody, Dr. Raymond A. Jr. *Life After Life*. NY: Bantam Books, 1975.

Sheldrake, Rupert. *Dogs That Know When Their Owners are Coming Home: And Other Unexplained Powers of Animals*. New York: Crown Publishers, 1999.

Talbot, Michael. *The Holographic Universe*. NY: Harper Collins Publishers, 1991.

GETTYSBURG GHOST INVESTIGATION CHECKLIST

Location:

Investigator(s):

Brief History of Site (Include names of historical individuals associated with the site. If a building is involved, include interviews with owners or residents regarding paranormal events):

Date:

Time: Start_____Finish_____

Weather: Rainy____Fog____Snow_____Clear_____

Temperature:

Humidity: Dry___; Damp___

Moon Phase:

Sunset/Sunrise Time:

Solar Activity:

Equipment & Methods Used:

Video (Type):_____Night shot used?_____

Cameras (Digital or other type):_____

Audio (Digital or magnetic tape):_____

Remote Temperature Meter (Thermal Scanner):_____

Results: (See also attachments with photos)

Time:_____Event:

Time:_____Event:

Time:_____Event:

Time:_____Event:

Time:_____Event:

GETTYSBURG GHOST INVESTIGATION CHECKLIST

Location:

Investigator(s):

Brief History of Site (Include names of historical individuals associated with the site. If a building is involved, include interviews with owners or residents regarding paranormal events):

Date:

Time: Start_____Finish_____

Weather: Rainy____Fog____Snow_____Clear_____

Temperature:

Humidity: Dry___; Damp___

Moon Phase:

Sunset/Sunrise Time:

Solar Activity:

Equipment & Methods Used:

Video (Type):_____Night shot used?_____

Cameras (Digital or other type):_____

Audio (Digital or magnetic tape):_____

Remote Temperature Meter (Thermal Scanner):_____

Results: (See also attachments with photos)

Time:_____Event:

Time:_____Event:

Time:_____Event:

Time:_____Event:

Time:_____Event:

GETTYSBURG GHOST INVESTIGATION CHECKLIST

Location:

Investigator(s):

Brief History of Site (Include names of historical individuals associated with the site. If a building is involved, include interviews with owners or residents regarding paranormal events):

Date:

Time: Start_____ Finish_____

Weather: Rainy____ Fog____ Snow_____ Clear_____

Temperature:

Humidity: Dry___ ; Damp___

Moon Phase:

Sunset/Sunrise Time:

Solar Activity:

Equipment & Methods Used:

Video (Type):_____ Night shot used?_____

Cameras (Digital or other type):_____

Audio (Digital or magnetic tape):_____

Remote Temperature Meter (Thermal Scanner):_____

Results: (See also attachments with photos)

Time:_____**Event:**

Time:_____**Event:**

Time:_____**Event:**

Time:_____**Event:**

Time:_____**Event:**

Mark Nesbitt was born in Lorain, Ohio, and graduated from Baldwin-Wallace College with a BA in English Literature. He worked for the National Park Service as a Ranger/Historian for five years and then became a Licensed Battlefield Guide. During his tenure with the National Park Service, he had the opportunity to spent time in nearly every historic house on the Park and actually lived in four of the historic homes. Living in Gettysburg since 1971 has given him a unique "insider" perspective from which to write this book.

Mr. Nesbitt published the first book in the popular *Ghosts of Gettysburg* series in 1991. The *Ghosts of Gettysburg* Series received the National Paranormal Award for "Best True Hauntings Collection" and "Best 'Local Haunt' Guidebook."

The *Ghosts of Gettysburg* stories have been seen, and/or heard, on The History Channel, A&E, The Discovery Channel, The Travel Channel, Unsolved Mysteries, and Coast to Coast AM.

Other books by Mark Nesbitt:

Ghosts of Gettysburg
More Ghosts of Gettysburg
Ghosts of Gettysburg III
Ghosts of Gettysburg IV
Ghosts of Gettysburg V
Ghosts of Gettysburg VI

If the South Won Gettysburg

35 Days to Gettysburg: The Campaign Diaries of Two American Enemies

Rebel Rivers: A Guide to Civil War Sites on the Potomac, Rappahannock, York, and James

Saber and Scapegoat: J.E.B. Stuart and the Gettysburg Controversy

Through Blood and Fire: The Selected Civil War Papers of Major General Joshua Chamberlain

To order any of Mark Nesbitt's books, or for more information on *The Ghosts of Gettysburg Candlelight Walking Tours®*, please visit:

www.ghostsofgettysburg.com

Or write to:
Second Chance Publications
P. O. Box 3126
Gettysburg, PA 17325
info@secondchancepublications.com